BOOK OF
Making Magic on the New and Full Moon
CEREMONIES

AMANDA RIEGER GREEN, MPH
TIFFANY HARELIK, MA

Spellbound
PUBLISHERS

BOOK OF
Making Magic on the New and Full Moon
CEREMONIES

AMANDA RIEGER GREEN, MPH
TIFFANY HARELIK, MA

Amanda Rieger Green, MPH, RYT and Tiffany Harelik, MA, RYT are business partners at Wise Skies Advice, an astrology and numerology business and Spellbound Publishers, a metaphysical book publishing company. www.WiseSkiesAdvice.com + www.SpellboundPublishers.com

Spellbound
PUBLISHERS

Library of Congress Control Number: 2019905807
Paperback ISBN 978-0-9977349-9-7

Contents

Dedication

We dedicate this book to anyone who wants to make a change in their life.

The ceremony templates offered here are not the magic—you are the magic. When you have a true desire for change, a willingness to get into right action, and an open heart, spiritual blessings are always sure to follow.

Acknowledgements

We would like to thank our teachers, mentors, family, friends, and supporters who have inspired this project.

The Wise Skies and Spellbound audiences: We genuinely appreciate your interest in bettering your lives and working together to increase healing, light, and love.

Terry Hobbs Heller, PhD: Our high priestess of editing, and Tiff's aunt Tootie.

Lisa Rieger: Our wise woman of words, and Amanda's mother.

Our spiritual advisors: Adrienne Cobb, Deborah Carter Mastelotto, Kim Le Blanc, Russell Forsyth, Aurora Garcia-Saqui, Barbara Marciniak and Ellen Crabaugh.

Our beloved pets and animal guides who passed during the writing of this book: Levi, Justice, Buck, and Ouisie.

Our supportive family: Dennis, Lisa, Jimmy, Patsy, Callie, Brighton, and Caleb - we love you.

Ourselves: Last but not least, we wish to acknowledge each other. We have answered a heart's calling to collaborate on many projects together, and we are proud of what we have accomplished within the pages of this book. We are stronger and wiser together, and we appreciate the opportunity to be of service.

"That, I think, is the power of ceremony. It marries the mundane to the sacred. The Water turns to wine; the coffee to a prayer."

— Robin Wall Kimmerer, *Braiding Sweetgrass: Indigenous Wisdom, Scientific Knowledge, and the Teachings of Plants*

Foreword

Beth Ebbing Johnson, Herbalist
Owner of Sacred Moon Herbs

We humans have been creating rituals and ceremonies around the changing of seasons and Moon phases since the beginning of time as a way to help us stay grounded and connected to our surroundings. Whether simple, or long and elaborate, ceremonies give us a sense of belonging to something greater than ourselves.

For me, ceremony is a way of life. Literally. I start each morning brewing my favorite jasmine green tea, then light a stick of herbal incense and draw an inspirational card to read from an oracle deck. Later, I will choose special crystals to take with me, and put on sacred seed jewelry to wear for the day. On my way out the front door I ring two little brass bells and then off I go venturing into the world.

There are endless ways you can bring ceremony and rituals into your life. This magickal book is packed full of sacred ceremonies you can create. You'll gain a greater knowledge of the Moon phases and different ways to celebrate the zodiac wheel. You'll begin to look at the world in a new light. I've included one of my personal ceremonies for you. Here's to creating your own magick!

Releasing What Doesn't Serve Me Bath

Contributed by Beth Ebbing Johnson, Herbalist

It's true that some days are harder than others. When I feel the sorrows of the planet a little more, the loss of a loved one or extra exhausted, an herbal bath how I shift my energy. I customize each bath for what has happened to make me feel this way, so each bath is slightly different. As you absorb more of the teachings from the flower and gem essences, crystals, aromatherapy, energy and herbal medicines, you can grow this ceremonial bath to fit your changing emotional needs.

You might have herbs like chamomile or rosemary growing around you or leaves from a tree you love. Whenever possible, use a sprinkle of fresh plants in your baths. Fresh herbs & flowers just adds a bit more healing magick to your baths.

Here's an enchanted bath base recipe to start your healing journey. I only recommend organic ingredients.

1 cup Epsom Salt
1 cup Sea Salt of your choice
1 teaspoon powder red rose petals or fresh petals you grow yourself
1 teaspoon powdered sage or fresh leaves you grow yourself
1 teaspoon powdered holy basil or fresh leaves you grow yourself
7 drops quintessential essences
1 tablespoon carrier oil (apricot, jojoba, coconut oil)
3 drops bergamot essential oil
3 drops eucalyptus essential oil
1 drop organic neroli essential oil
1 clear quartz
1 rose quartz
1 carnelian

Whisk the dry ingredients together in a glass or ceramic bowl. Place a carrier oil, essential oils and essences into a small bowl and mix thoroughly. Pour the small bowl of oils into the glass bowl of dried herbs and whisk together until well blended. Your bath magick preparation is complete.

Fill your tub with warm Water, add ingredients, infuse intentions, climb in and soak for 30 minutes (at the very least). If you don't have a bath tub, cut this recipe in half and use it as a foot bath.

Beth Ebbing Johnson, Herbalist & owner of Sacred Moon Herbs

Beth's love of herbs and nature came from growing up on her family's farm where she spent days playing in the woods and going on walks with her family collecting hickory nuts, walnuts, acorns, morel mushrooms, and wildflowers. Bluebells are her favorite of them all. Beth holds an Associates Degree in

Holistic Healthcare along with a specialty in Western Herbalism from the Southwest Institute of Healing Arts (SWIHA). She has studied many holistic modalities including Herbalism, Hypnotherapy, Aromatherapy, Reflexology, Polarity, Astrology, Chakra, and Meditation practices. She graduated with

After becoming a certified Herbalist, Beth worked with Whole Foods Market, Desert Sage Herbs, Dr. Hauschka, the Herb Bar, and several other herbal companies. After almost a decade, the dream of being an owner of an herb shop came true, and Sacred Moon Herbs opened her doors in 2012.

Sacred Moon Herbs

Sacred Moon Herbs is located in Dripping Springs Texas, a quaint town about 20 miles west of Austin. Sacred Moon is a place for one to start or continue your healing journey. We carry over 200 organic bulk herbs, teas and spices. We also offer around 50 organic essential oils. On top of those swirling aromas, we burn sage and Shoyeido's plant based incenses. We hope and feel that you receive whatever blessing is meant to be for you.

"Everything is ceremony in the wild garden of childhood."

— Pablo Neruda, Nobel Prize winner, Chilean poet-diplomat and politician

Introduction

Ceremony creates new reality.

Something real happens after you participate in a ceremony. The energy inside you and around you changes. Quantum science has proven that joining a clear intention or thought (electrical charge) with a feeling or emotion (magnetic charge) creates a new electro-magnetic force, a new reality.

Ceremony does exactly that.

Ceremonies are both personal and universal.

There are time honored traditions that bind us together through celebrations of birth, graduation, marriage, and death. Other ceremonies are quite private, wherein one comes up with their own symbols or actions in reverence for a precious wish.

Whether within a group or on your own, a ceremony sends a clear message of intention to the Universe: you mean business.

Every two weeks, like clockwork, the Moon offers us a unique opportunity.

The New Moon is a time to work with Spirit, or God, and our spiritual guides or tribes of light, in planting seeds of intention for new growth. Conversely, the Full Moon is a time to work with our Spirit teams in aligning with closure, or an end of a cycle.

Consciously creating ceremonies based on the lunar cycle is one way we can get back in sync with the natural rhythms of our planet.

How? It's simpler than you might think. The human body is over 50% Water—the Moon influences the tides in the oceans, and it influences you as well.

When you understand the elements associated with the astrological sign the Moon is in, you add a powerful ingredient in the secret sauce of creating ceremonies.

The alchemical concept is true: As above, so below.

You know how it works: your outer world is a reflection of your inner world. In the same way, your inner perspectives, beliefs, and intentions shape and shift your day to day experience.

Are your feet doing what your mouth is saying it wants? Are you being completely honest with yourself when considering your wishes, goals, and actions?

The lunar cycles are a good time to check in with your motives and desires, and measure them against your daily actions. Remember that you are a creatrix, a powerful creator.

Ceremony brings us closer to the divine. It shortens the distance between the wish and the wisher.

A ritual offers an opportunity to connect with the sacred for the purpose of honoring a rite of passage, celebrating an experience, or for effecting a change.

We all have the stroke of the magician when we create ceremony.

We can optimize the lunar cycles by knowing more about the phase of the Moon, the sign of the zodiac in which it occurs, and the numerology involved. But, ultimately, it's your unique connection with God or the Spirit of your own understanding that assists you in creating the practical magic of ceremony and stirring the deep Waters of change.

Ceremonies aren't just for the ancients—they are one of the best tools we have in modern society to bridge human and spiritual worlds.

Ceremonies send signals to the Universe that we are aware, awake, and intentional - that we want to co-create our lives with a divine plan.

This book helps you turn the ordinary into the extraordinary through creating your own ceremonies.

"The purpose of any ceremony is to build stronger relationships or bridge the distance between our cosmos and us. The research that we do as Indigenous people is a ceremony that allows us a raised level of consciousness and insight into our world. Through going forward together with open minds and good hearts we have uncovered the nature of this ceremony."

- Shawn Wilson, *Research is Ceremony*

PART 1

Ceremonies 101

Why Do We Need Ceremonies?

Ceremonies are cultural traditions that have spanned thousands of years. They are practiced for a variety of reasons, using a variety of customs, over different lengths of time. While some are conducted as public celebrations, ceremonies can also be created privately to set intentions or to work on spiritual growth.

We conduct ceremonies at special times throughout human life including baptisms, bar mitzvahs, birthdays, graduation, marriage, major awards, retirement, and funerals. We also conduct ceremonies as special community events such as ribbon cuttings, inducting someone into political office, and opening ceremonies at sports games.

Ceremonies are comprised of a few main components: spoken word or song, particular actions, and particular timing. For example, there is often a standard process (singing the *Star Spangled Banner* or walking down the aisle), followed by a declaration ("Play ball!" or "I now pronounce you husband and wife!").

Ceremonies bring people together to mark a milestone, or mark a change of events. While public ceremony has a format that is generated through tradition or protocol, we often make up the rules as we go along in personal or private ceremony. In this book, we offer a template for you to use in personal ceremonies to incorporate the four elements (Fire, Earth, Air, and Water) as well as astrology and numerology. We included the elements because of their powerful presence in nature, and included ideas for incorporating astrology and numerology because of their power in our personal lives.

Why do we need our own personal ceremonies? For one, a ceremony offers a physical way to connect with the divine. It is a definitive act for showing the Universe that you want to effect a change or commemorate a special moment.

Instead of wishful thinking, getting your wishes out of your head and into the Earth realm triggers a karmic call and response with the Universe.

By being in acceptance of what is—while also being ready for a change—we can offer our heart's desires to God in a personal ceremony and truly trust in divine right timing for the wishes to unfold organically.

The emotions of gratitude, devotion, and humility that are evoked during ceremonies provide a sacred heart connection to the spiritual power of co-creation.

What Should You Wish For?

Some people think of "wishing" as a pie-in-the-sky, frivolous thing to do. Nothing could be further from the truth. Your dreams and aspirations are what pull you into the future—what lead you to accomplish something with your life—and wishing for something is the very essence of hope.

So, what are some of the things you hope for? What do you want? And, how do you decide? And how do you ask for what you want? These questions are addressed in this book in a very special way—through ceremony.

And done the right way—with heart and mind in true coherence—these ceremonies *work*.

But, there's a trick to it: the ceremonies planned here are only for the good, and only for the authentic you—not for anyone else.

So, how could wishes go wrong? There's nothing wrong with wishing and setting intentions, and asking for Spiritual guidance. But here's where it can go wrong:

1. **Wishing for or against other people is a no**. Wishing for someone else to do something you want is manipulation—it isn't good, it doesn't work, and it isn't what this book is about. This book is about *you* and *your* desires and *your* wishes for *your own life*.

   Everyone has their own life and their own path and unique wishes. Including you. It is the premise of the ceremonies in this book that you will frame your wishes only for yourself and let the Universe sort it out where others in your life are concerned . . . with one caveat: wishing or setting an intention solely for the healing or good fortune of another is altruistic and carries the overlight of grace.

When you have strong feelings or emotions that involve other people, it can be tricky to discern how to wish. Keep in mind that you are called to use your intentions wisely. For example: you're in love with someone who doesn't seem to love you back. Instead of wishing to 'make them love me,' perhaps you want to wish to feel more love in your life. Look deeply inside to discern the best path for love wishes. You may find that the true desire may be simply to love yourself, first—to love your own life! As another example, maybe there is a pesky person stirring the pot in your relationship. Instead of wishing for them to 'go away,' consider wishing to experience mutual love and respect, along with healthy boundaries in all of your relationships.

Reframing your desire in a way that magnetizes the feeling tone of what you'd like to experience is a healthy way to ask for what you want, without manipulating or controlling others.

2. **Wishing with impure motives doesn't work.** What motivates your desire in making a wish? Anger with yourself or others, judging yourself or others, fear, arrogance—these are all emotions that carry negative or low vibrations. Negative vibes do not work well as root motivators for setting an intention for a ceremony—nor do they work well for anything else, for that matter.

Examine your motives honestly, and seek spiritual guidance for discernment in finding the motive behind your true heart's desire. Once you identify your motive, you have the fundamental piece for effective wish-making.

For example, you're feeling badly about your weight or self-image and you want to wish for an improved physical appearance. You might think of an initial wish: "I want to feel better about having a less than perfect figure." The root of this desire is judging yourself and therefore it is detrimental to your wish. Consider reframing the motive with positive, loving, believable emotions having to do with loving yourself instead of judging yourself. In this example, you might use something like this: "I want to feel good about taking care of myself with healthy eating habits and a regular yoga practice."

3. **Wishing for something when you're not truly "feeling it" doesn't work either.** If you're wishing for something because you think you're *supposed* to wish for it, that's actually self-deceiving and dishonest. And it sends mixed messages into the Universe. Nothing really works when you know you're not being honest with yourself. An example is feeling like you should wish for a "steady job" but deep down you don't really want to work 9-5.

   A more authentic wish might be: "Help me get in touch with the part of me that is resistant to a traditional 9-5 job so I can have a greater understanding of myself and my highest good." Or, phrase it as a specific intention that you know you really want, such as: "By December 31st, 2020, I am able to support myself using my talents for music and writing." And a third option might look like this: "I am willing to create more abundance in my life. I enjoy feeling stable and secure in non-traditional ways. Money flows to me and through me more easily than ever before."

4. **Wishing for something but, deep down, harboring the belief that none of this is going to work *really* doesn't work.** It's a fact: your beliefs govern everything you do. If you don't believe you deserve money, or that you have to be a certain weight or look a certain way to attract love, or that you're just "unlucky," or that wishes and intentions don't work for you, you will sabotage yourself every time.

   Look at it this way: whatever you think and believe has gotten you where you are today! If you like your life just the way it is and don't need or want to change anything, that is perfectly fine. This book, however, is for those who want to experience some kind of change in their life or circumstances.

   The truth is, you are a product of your thoughts, beliefs, and desires. Whatever you put out there as a bona fide belief or heartfelt desire is what the Universe works to bring to you. If you think you are not worthy of a true love, or that there is no one out there just for you, then sure enough no one comes. It takes rigorous self-authenticity - knowing yourself and your own inner goodness of *being*, just as you are - and a sustained desire to promote a change in your life. It's not as hard as you might think. It just takes *doing and feeling and believing.*

Ceremonial Elements:
Fire, Earth, Air, Water

Earth My Body
Water My Blood
Air My Breath
and Fire My Spirit

—Native American Chant

The Native American chant *Earth My Body* is common to many circles and acknowledges we are all intricately connected to the living Earth. It's a song of self-awareness, and an acknowledgement of our space within Space.

The four elements offer a template for getting intentions out of our head, and into our reality. We use all four elements in our ceremonies as symbols of transmutation.

Fire signifies life, provision, protection, and love.

Of the four elements, the sacredness of Fire is the most universal element of all spiritual traditions. Consider that our ancestors spent much of the day cooking with Fire. Fire was the vital force that allowed them to prepare food for the table. They also spent time in gatherings around the red and purple flames of a communal Fire at the end of the day, bringing warmth and a measure of safety at night.

A candle flame is a living symbol of the Fire of the Divine, or Spirit. It draws our attention, touches the heart, and connects us to the light of our common origin.

Fire gazing clears stress and negativity in your cells and our spiritual aura. When you look into a Fire with an open heart, it sets the tone for connecting with Spirit. A channel to the divine opens. By using Fire in ceremonies, you are more easily able to receive divine thoughts. After Fire gazing, you will feel relaxed, refreshed, and at your energetic best.

Fire may be the most common element in terms of ceremony, but the other three elements—Air, Earth, and Water—have equally important roles in the balance, grace, and flow of of ritual and ceremony.

Earth signifies stability, practicality, and renewal.

Using Earth elements in rituals and ceremonies help to "ground" and stabilize you and your intentions. Examples of this include burying intentions in the ground and planting seeds in the garden. Burying material or planting and giving something back to the Earth allows the Earth to mulch and transform the energy, creating life, even life out of death.

Incorporating Earth elements such as drumming also helps balance your Root chakra and create stability, well-being, and trust. Using Earth elements in rituals and in everyday life offers us a sense of stability, practicality, and the fruits of a job well done. Getting outside, taking your shoes off and grounding your feet on the bare Earth, or hugging a tree and feeling its life-force coincide with yours, can attune your natural, biological rhythms in resonance with the cosmos.

Air signifies the mental realm.

Incorporating breath work, mindfulness, and music are three common ways to add the Air element in ceremonies. Using singing bowls, wind chimes, prayers, songs, words, breathing exercises, and spoken blessings are all ideas for bringing more Air into your ceremonies.

Air is how we communicate and articulate our thoughts, words, feelings, needs, wishes, and desires. It is through our intentions that we create a dialogue between ourselves, others, and the universe. Words empower and also can disempower. Thus, it is through consciously using the element of Air that we breathe life into being and co-create our reality. It is our choice to be conscious co-creators via thoughts and communications of integrity.

Water signifies flow, emotional clarity, and intuition.

Using Water in ceremony helps purify, bless, cleanse, and renew. For example, holy Water is used in baptism or christening, or steam is used to purify in Native American sweat lodge rituals. A bath or shower is in an ideal space for cleansing your physical, mental, emotional, and spiritual self, creating a flow for purer energies.

Water is a powerful conductor, carrying both positive and negative frequencies and energies. Water amplifies the ebb and flow of thoughts, feelings, and the unseen energy field around you.

Fire, Earth, Air, and Water are the basic elements to include in each ceremony you plan. But before you do anything else, the first order of creating ceremony is to establish a sacred space.

Sacred Space

"Each place is the right place—the place where
I now am can be a sacred space."

- Ravi Ravindra, *The Wisdom of Patanjali's Yoga
Sutras: A New Translation and Guide*

What is sacred space and why does it need to be opened?

Sacred space is any place you distinguish to perform ceremonies. Opening sacred space creates a portal or intentional vibration within the area where you are conducting ceremony. The act of opening sacred space also conjures an element of safety and protection. Think of it as opening a prayer field wherein you are supported by many great beings, and where great potential exists.

Does sacred space need to be closed?

Yes. It is equally important to close sacred space. Once the ceremony is over, it's important to seal the energy. You can do this simply by acknowledging the same elements you invoked in opening the space.

Process for opening and closing sacred space

We offer different ways to open and close sacred space throughout the ceremonies in this book. Specifically, we offer opening and closing prayers in the New Moon and Full Moon sections. Here is a simple template you can use to make up your own way to open and close sacred space. It can be as simple as an opening and closing prayer you say in your heart before and after each ceremony.

Opening Sacred Space

Before you begin your ceremony, you may open the space like this:

1. Acknowledge with reverence (e.g., bow, look or nod in the direction, signal with the hand, etc.) to the six directions: South, West, North, East, the Earth below, and the Sky above.

2. Thank the sacred Spirit or spirit team you are working with and welcome them to the space: God or Great Spirit, the Moon and planetary bodies, other spiritual beings such as the galactic councils of light, archangels, the angels of the great central Sun, your guardian angel, ascended masters (Jesus, Buddha, Saints), deceased family members or ancestors, and so on.

3. Visualize a channel of white liquid light flowing from a spot above your head, through the crown of your head, down through your spine, and then down into the Earth. This visualization is to clear your physical, emotional, and spiritual body. Visualize this light becoming fluorescent in cleansing your DNA and the cells of your body and then shining it's unique rays out from your heart into the world.

Closing Sacred Space

After your ceremony, you may close the space in a similar fashion.

1. Acknowledge with reverence and gratitude each of the six directions you used to open the space.

2. Acknowledge and thank the spiritual beings who attended you during the ceremony, feeling appreciation for their presence.

3. Honor your Higher Self with acknowledgement and gratitude for being present to you and for the power of co-creation.

The Lunar Cycle

"Astrology is a Language. If you understand this language, The Sky Speaks to You."

—Dane Rudhyar, *A Handbook for the Humanistic Astrologer*

Why do we use the lunar cycle to make wishes and set goals? Author and syndicated astrologer Jan Spiller states that incorporating the moon with intentions is an ancient practice, and that knowing there is power in wishes or intentions has been handed down through the ages. Spiller notes that even children "know to make a wish on a falling star or a passing hay truck." A child instinctively looks at the Moon and believes it is a connection for making dreams come true. Wishing focuses the mind at a "magic moment," and can "transform the desires of the heart into material reality."

Spiller reminds us that wishes made with faith *do* come true. In this book we show that tying wishes to specific astrological events during phases of the Moon is the secret ingredient for creating effective ceremonies. It's helpful to understand the significance behind the different phases of the Moon when mapping out the intentions powering your ceremonies. Although we focus on the New and Full Moon phases, we invite you to be the author of your own destiny *at any time* of your choosing by creating your own magic, honoring your wishes and dreams—and making them come true—through ceremony.

New Moon: Make a Wish

The New Moon signifies new beginnings and is a great time to set intentions, plant seeds or ideas, and start something new. This is the phase of unconditional love and light. Trust your instincts during this phase as you're likely to feel more alive and in tune with your body wisdom than in any other phase. In her book *New Moon Astrology*, Spiller teaches the importance of making wishes within the first 8 hours of the time the New Moon is exact. This phase is when the Moon is positioned between the Earth and the Sun, making it invisible. In the Sky, you'll see a dark silhouette of a circle where the Moon is in shadow. Luna is not illuminated during this phase—there is total darkness—so it's also a great time to stargaze and ponder your dreams.

First Quarter Moon: Make a Commitment

This yang or active phase engenders decision making, determination, and commitment to action. In the Sky, you'll see exactly half of the Moon illuminated. This is a good time for finding courage and inner strength. The first quarter moon is not for shying away from life - it's a time to learn through new experiences. And it is a period for being aware of your reactions: how do you show up when you meet your "edge" in life? While regular meditation can help slow your emotional reactions during this phase, ceremony during this time can support spiritual growth and promote inspiration.

Full Moon: Celebrate Completion

During the Full Moon you can find freedom from struggle. This phase signifies the completion of a cycle, endings, and closure. Think of the Full Moon as a time to harvest blessings and to express gratitude from the past few weeks, or current challenges, or previous season. If you notice people are more touchy than usual it is because Full Moon is a time when the inner and outer worlds are split. There can be a sense of loneliness or a feeling that things are irreconcilable. Remember that we are always in a state of impermanence, and in dealing with our emotions and perspectives there is the conventional wisdom that "this too shall pass." The entire Moon is illuminated during this phase, and standing under it you can feel quite magical in its bright, beautiful light.

Last Quarter Moon: Trust the Process

During the Last Quarter phase it's time to get out of the mix and look at things more objectively—become the wise observer. In the Sky you'll see exactly half of the Moon illuminated. This yin, or internal phase, signifies receptivity and a willingness to trust, to surrender, and to let things take their course. This is a moment to call on your faith, and to know that all is truly well.

Using the Moon sign to create themes

In this book, we give several recipes for ceremonies based on the astrological sign the Moon is in (whether New or Full). Creating ceremony in this way taps into the archetypes of the different zodiac signs, and offers ideas on specific themes you can work with.

How do I know what phase and sign the Moon is in?

The Moon's cycle is about 29 ½ days. The four phases of the Moon are determined in relationship to the Sun. Each phase lasts approximately one week. Luna moves in the order of the zodiac, spending two to three days in each sign: Aries, Taurus, Gemini, Cancer, Leo, Virgo, Libra, Scorpio, Sagitarrius, Capricorn, Aquarius, and Pisces. If working with Moon signs and phases is new to you, you can find more information the old-fashioned way—such as in the Farmer's Almanac—or in a "new"-fashioned way through the Wise Skies digital calendar, or through various free online sources.

Because we tend to rely on what sign and phase the Moon is in when conducting ceremony, it can be fun to explore a little more about how we incorporate astrology into our daily lives by learning about the basic principles and archetypes in the Sky—the planets, signs, and houses.

Astrology Basics

"Astrology is one of the earliest attempts made by man
to find the order hidden behind or within the confusing
and apparent chaos that exists in the world."

—Karen Hamaker-Zondag, Author and Psychological Astrologist

Astrology is the study of planets and celestial bodies in motion, and these are interpreted by astrologers as having an influence on human psychology and the natural world. We can use astrology to look at where the planets are at any given time—such as at birth—to determine personality as well as windows of opportunity and optimal timing. Astrology is a lifetime study, but by understanding a few basic foundations, you will be able to use the cosmos to create beautiful intentions and ceremonies.

Astrologer and author Chris Fischer states that "(a)strology is one of the oldest and most accurate tools known to mankind." Astrology is an ancient science that involves a little artistic interpretation. You've often heard the phrase "the stars must be aligned." And it's true. There are certain times that are ideal to execute a wish, set up meetings for success, start new ventures, harvest the fruits of your labor, and put something to rest.

There are many branches and lineages to studying astrology: Vedic, Hellenistic, Esoteric, Transcendental, Chinese, and Western are a few. Within each tradition, there are as many different ways to interpret personalities and make use of the phases of the Moon as there are astrologers. Translating the motion of the Skies into practical advice involves both science and intuitive work. For the purposes of this book, we pull from the Western approach, and yet honor all scholars of the Skies.

Personal Astrology: The Natal Chart

"We are born at a given moment, in a given place, and, like vintage years of wine, we have the qualities of the year and the season of which we are born. Astrology does not lay claim to anything more."

- Carl Jung, Swiss Psychiatrist and Psychoanalyst,
Founder of Analytic Psychology

The natal chart is a wheel that illustrates where the planets were in the Sky at the time of your birth. This is why knowing your exact birth time is so important to astrologers. Even a slight one-minute difference could result in a planet landing in a different sign or house, creating different life aspects, and resulting in a completely different interpretation of life potentialities.

The natal chart is often where we start learning about astrology because it's the study of ourselves. This chart offers clues about our personalities and personal rhythms. Consider your natal chart a script for the great movie of your life. Whether you read the script or not, the natal chart is a great place to begin to understand your unique soul blueprint and why you operate the way you do.

The Planets

The first thing to look at in your natal chart are the planets. They are the actors in this great movie of your life. The planets represent personalities and specific character traits. Their energies are neither good nor bad. But, depending on how they are placed within your chart (the aspects), you may experience a range of lower to higher vibrations with each of them. Knowing which sign each of the planets in your chart is in gives you a fun new personal development tool to explore.

Some planets move fast and change signs every few days. Others take hundreds of years to change signs. This can explain why some traits or passions describe a whole generation of people, and other traits and passions are specific to an individual.

SUN
The Sun's placement describes your personality and the way you approach life. Themes: Self, Central Theme, Identity, Vitality, Life Force, Confidence, Ego

MOON
The Moon's placement describes your emotional needs and how you relate to others.

Themes: Receptivity, Emotion, Intuition, Childhood, Parents, Familial Influences

MERCURY

Mercury's placement describes the way you think and process information.

Themes: Thoughts, Communications, Details, Intricate Systems, Processing, Advertising

VENUS

Venus' placement describes the way you like to give and receive love and how you feel worth.

Themes: Beauty, Self-worth, Love, Money, Luxury, Value, Creativity

MARS

Mars' placement describes where you have a lot of energy and drive.

Themes: Drive, Determination, Aggression, Anima, Anger, War, Assertiveness, Action

JUPITER

Jupiter's placement describes where you're lucky and where you seek growth.

Themes: Luck, Expansion, Dismutation, Growth, Abundance, Overseas Travel, Laws, Publishing

SATURN

Saturn's placement describes where you're committed, and what type of career is ideal for you.

Themes: Work, Career, Stability, Constriction, Karma, Boundaries, Discipline, Commitments

URANUS

Uranus' placement describes where you see a lot of turnover and movement.

Themes: Revolution, Change, Shock and Awe, Brilliant Ideas

NEPTUNE

Neptune's placement describes where things tend to dissolve or are elusive.

Themes: Entertainment, Dreams, Meditation, Delusion, Illusion, Fantasy, Music, Art

PLUTO

Pluto's placement describes your biggest opportunities for healing and transformation.

Themes: Transformation, Phoenix Rising, Subconscious, Depth, Power, Death, Sex

CHIRON

Chiron's placement describes a wound you've had to overcome and where you can be of service to others.

Themes: Wounding, Healing, Teaching, Acceptance, Journeying

The Signs of the Zodiac

The planets are each located within one of the twelve signs of the zodiac. Consider the zodiac the wardrobe of the movie that is unfolding. Some of the planets are very comfortable in some signs (or "cosmic clothes"), and very uncomfortable in others. This creates different energy. It's the difference between how you feel and behave when you're in your most comfortable sweatshirt and pajama pants versus dressing in formal wear for a special occasion. Consider how you feel if you're in your sweats and someone walks in the room in a brilliant red dress or stunning tuxedo. It's not that much different with the planets.

The energy the planets exude is optimized when they are located in favorable signs. In other words, each planet has a 'favorite' sign wherein they are operating at optimal frequencies. They also have signs they tolerate, and signs where they are completely uncomfortable.

ARIES

Aries is a Fire sign ruled by Mars.

Traits: Pioneer, Firestarter, Hopeful, Bright-eyed, Hot-tempered, Headstrong

TAURUS

Taurus is an Earth sign ruled by Venus.

Traits: Dependable, Grounded, Stable, Resourceful, Stubborn, Sensual, Food-oriented

GEMINI

Gemini is an Air sign ruled by Mercury.

Traits: Capable, Multi-tasker, Intelligent, Analytic, Adaptable, Scattered, Social butterfly, Being of two minds

CANCER

Cancer is a Water sign ruled by the Moon.

Traits: Receptive, Empathic, Domestic, Security, Divine feminine, Stuffing emotions, Controlling

LEO

Leo is a Fire sign ruled by the Sun.

Traits: Passionate, Playful, Heart-centered, Leadership, Creative self-expression, Radiance, Vitality, Attention-seeking

VIRGO

Virgo is an Earth sign ruled by Mercury and Chiron.
Traits: Organized, Detail-oriented, Perfection, Discrimination, Standards, Healer, Data-oriented, Gardens, Critical, Judgmental, Hyper-focused, Approval-seeking

LIBRA

Libra is an Air sign ruled by Venus.
Traits: Balanced, Harmonic, Beautiful, FAir, Indecisive, Shallow

SCORPIO

Scorpio is a Water sign ruled by Mars and Pluto.
Traits: Magnetic, Intense, Unapologetic, Metamorphic, Sensual, Deep, Isolation-tendencies, Jealous, Vengeful, Powerful, Subconscious thinking

SAGITTARIUS

Sagittarius is a Fire sign ruled by Jupiter.
Traits: Playful, Cultured, Sporty, Philosophic, Adventurous, Travel-oriented, Worldly, Nonsensical, Everyone's best friend

CAPRICORN

Capricorn is an Earth sign ruled by Saturn.
Traits: Long-term planner, Natural leader, Ambitious, Healer, Integrity, Achievement-oriented, Disciplined, Resentful

AQUARIUS

Aquarius is an Air sign ruled by Saturn and Uranus.
Traits: Brilliant, Inventive, Unpredictable, Unreliable, Oriented towards the Collective/Group, Detached, Controlling

PISCES

Pisces ia a Water sign ruled by Jupiter and Neptune.
Traits: Intuitive, ClAirvoyant, Selfless, Sacrificial, Charitable, Tolerant, Compassionate, Mystical, Deceptive, Delusional, Escape-artist

The Houses

In Western astrology, everyone has 12 houses in their natal chart. Consider the houses as the locations or sets of this great movie in your birth chart. The movie unfolds differently for each of us depending on the location of the planets across the houses of the zodiac. Each house is comprised of 30 degrees. Multiply this by the 12 houses and you get 360 degrees total to create the wheel. Because the Earth turns, it will face each of the 360 degrees of the zodiac in a 24-hour period. The cusp is the first point or threshold of the house coming up, and acts as a preview to the energy present in that house.

1ST HOUSE: Self, Ego, How I Present Myself

2ND HOUSE: Money, Values, Self-Worth

3RD HOUSE: Communication, Siblings, Mentality, Processing Information

4TH HOUSE: Home, Family, Nourishment, Living Space

5TH HOUSE: Play, Fun, Workshops, Heart

6TH HOUSE: Service, Gardens + Herbs, Vocation, Healing Work

7TH HOUSE: Relationship, Significant Partnership, Sacred Union

8TH HOUSE: Shared Resources, Endings + Eclipses, Sex, Death, Taxes

9TH HOUSE: Philosophy, Publishing, Overseas Travel

10TH HOUSE: Career, Social Status, Reputations

11TH HOUSE: Friends, Social Networks, Benevolent Forces

12TH HOUSE: Subconscious Mind, Hidden Prisons, Mystery

The aspects and transits

The aspects or spatial relationships of the planets in your birth chart offer another piece of the plot. These aspects are the sacred geometric shapes that offer more information on how the planetary energies interact with each other. Some aspects are favorable, some are neutral, and some offer challenges.

Transits are the effects of a moving planet on your personal chart. Studying transits offers an explanation of the ebb and flow of major changes and day to day ups and downs in your life. It also offers one reason in a sea of variables as to why you might be having a really great day while your friend might be having a crummy one. The bottom line is that the cosmos affects each of us differently at any given time.

Astrology for Ceremony: The Wisdom of the Sky

In the above section, you learned about the natal chart—the basic blueprint of your personality and how you navigate the world. Everyone's natal chart is unique, but we all live under the same day-to-day cosmic conditions when the planets and Moon change signs, when they form positive or challenging aspects with each other, etc. These cosmic conditions are what astrologers use to write the monthly forecast—a useful astrological weather report you can work with to create ceremony.

The ceremonies in this book are not specific to your horoscope sign—they are specific only to what is going on in the Sky at large.

If you're new to this, you may be thinking "I'm an Aries," and then geek out on the Aries New Moon and Aries Full Moon ceremonies that are provided as sample illustrations. You can certainly have fun reading those and identify with some of the major themes! However, we ALL live under the Aries New/Full Moon, and we can ALL take advantage of creating ceremony under this unique Moon.

Yes, you will need to know what sign the Moon is in to best use the ceremonies in this book. But don't worry—as stated earlier, there are many great resources that are free and online to help you know what sign the Moon is in. Once you know the sign the Moon is in, you're ready to use the ceremonies in this book.

The ceremonies we offer are simply guidelines. If you're feeling creative, you can use the tools we provide for coming up with your own ceremony. There are no rules for the tools, and the items are only for fun. It's your intention that matters most.

One of the tools we provide as an innovative feature of this book is Numerology, which is also part of the *Abundance Code Series* from Spellbound Publishers. You will find Numerology is truly unique tool for adding "special sauce" to the magic you will create with your ceremony. Prepare to be amazed.

Numerology Basics

"Numerology projections will fascinate you for your entire life."
— William Kennett, *Little Book of Destiny*

Numerology is the ancient study and practice based on the language of numbers. The quantifiable and established knowledge of vibrations and traits of the frequencies of different numbers offer us a view on life patterns and insights about ourselves and our experiences. When we understand the characteristics and behaviors of numbers they begin to tell a story about us as individuals, a special view on who we are and why we sometimes "feel" the way we do in a sense of place/time. Numerology helps to explain what we may be experiencing and helps connect the cosmic dots in our personal blueprints as unique humans in this lifetime—adding meaning, insights and navigational tips along the way.

Numerology is a special tool available for achieving what you want—such as changing a relationship, or creating more abundance, or for hitting the "reset" button in your life. The intentions provided for each of the basic number characteristics below can be useful in planning a ceremony using numerology.

First, there is a discussion of the "personality" properties of numbers. Next, there is an *intention* associated with each number. The intention is formulated to help smooth out potential negative aspects of a number's characteristics by boosting the positive counterparts.

Simply put, numbers are vibrations. The vibrations of the first nine cardinal numbers reflect personality traits that we all share. "Your" number is personal to you and is primarily based on your birth date. However, other numbers personally yours can also be relevant to your ceremony—such as your address, or the address of the ceremony, or date of the ceremony.

Understanding and using a numerology empowerment code in your ceremony can give a depth to your experience and outcome like no other tool. Like. No. Other.

And there's more. Take a look through the following special section on numerology. We teach you how to add up the numbers to find out not only your personal number, but also what your life path and attitude numbers are. Discover a whole new way of understanding your world by working with your numbers.

The building blocks of Numerology are the numbers 1-9

1: The Boss. The Individual. The Leader.
Energies and Traits: Drive, Confidence, Hustle, Independence, Yang, Masculine Energy, Goal-Driven, Organized, Focused, Pioneers, Inventors, Leaders
Quick intention for working with #1
I am open-minded, patient, and tolerant with myself and those around me.

2: Love the One You're With.
Energies and Traits: Balance, Harmony, Relationships, Feminine
Intuitive, Sensitive, Agreeable, Diplomatic, Flow, Trust, Peacemakers, Diplomats, Lovers
Quick intention for working with #2
I set and maintain healthy boundaries in all aspects of my life and relationships.

3: Attraction Rather Than Promotion.
Energies and Traits: Creativity, Pizazz, Charisma, Influence, Intuition
Optimism, Wonder, Sass, Entertainers, Artists, Social Mavens
Quick intention for working with #3
Rest, relaxation, and healthy self-care come naturally to me.

4: Organization Station.
Energies and Traits: Processes, Order, Tidiness, Consistency, Routine
Organization, Stability, Roots, Foundation, Discipline, Analysts, Engineers, Builders
Quick intention for working with #4
I am open-minded and willing to relinquish control, effortlessly allowing ease and flow into my life.

5: Lightning Strikes Twice.

Energies and Traits: Adventure, Adrenaline, Freedom, Entertainment, Flexibility, Independence, Momentum, Change, Action, Dynamic Force, Travelers, Promoters, Performers

Quick intention for working with #5

I am accountable and consistent and easily create balance in all areas of my life.

6: The Nester. The Nurturer. The Mother.

Energies and Traits: Comfort, Companionable, Nurturing, Nesting, Warm, Loving,
Authentic Connection, Unity, Service, Compassion, Protective, Health Care Practitioners, Counselors, Teachers

Quick intention for working with #6

I trust my voice and maintain interdependence in all relationships and situations.

7: The Passionate Path of Pursuit.

Energies and Traits: Wisdom, Seekers, Philosophers, Quest for Truth, Metaphysics,
Heightened Awareness, Knowledge, Analytical, Mystery, Mystics, Professors, Writers

Quick intention for working with #7

Collaboration, connection, and the sharing of ideas happens organically and feels enlightening.

8: Risk & Reward.

Energies and Traits: Infinity, Fluidity, Abundance, Power, Prosperity, Initiating, Momentum, Risk and Reward, Expansion, Entrepreneurs, Athletes, Brokers and Agents

Quick intention for working with #8

I experience peace and serenity in the present, while creating stability and consistency.

9: The Great Connection.

Energies and Traits: Experience, Integrity, Innate Wisdom, Connectedness, High Standards, Charisma, Influence, Relatable, Familiar, Humanitarians, CEOs, Spiritual Thought-Leaders

Quick intention for working with #9

Joy, happiness, and fun are priorities in my life and allow me to feel free.

Personal Numerology Basics

In Personal Numerology, the first two codes to learn are your Life Path number and your Attitude number. While the Life Path number provides information about your role in this lifetime, the Attitude number is a direct reflection of your personality—the way you look at the world—as well as how others perceive you. For those of you into astrology, think of the Life Path number as your Sun sign and the Attitude number as your Rising sign.

Life Path Number = Your Soul Purpose

The Life Path number is the most fundamental part of your numerology blueprint. It is the vibration you arrived with on this Earth and in this lifetime, and it's the vibration that you came to master and maneuver. Knowing your Life Path number will help you gain an understanding of how you limit and also free yourself. The Life Path number reflects your behaviors, attitudes, experience, and perspectives in life. It's the first number you want to know and understand. It is like your fingerprint—a number that is uniquely yours.

Calculating Your Life Path Number:
Sum up the month you were born + the day you were born + year you were born. Then, reduce it to a single digit number.
Example: Your birthdate is October 8th, 1980
The numbers to use are 10-08-1980
$1 + 0 + 0 + 8 + 1 + 9 + 8 + 0 = 27$
Reduce it to a single digit: $2 + 7 = 9$.
Your Life Path number is a 9.

Attitude Number = Your Attitude or Personality

The Attitude number is exactly what it says it is—your attitude, how other people see or perceive you. It's what you project or how you express yourself to the world around you. It's an *external personification* of you.

Calculating Your Attitude Number
Sum up the month you were born + the day you were born.
Then, reduce it down to a single digit number, if applicable.
Example: 10-08
$1 + 0 + 0 + 8 = 9$
Your Attitude Number is a 9

The Life Path number and the Attitude number are building blocks for your personal numerology blueprint, but there are so many more numbers to explore. You can calculate your Expression or Destiny (the numerology of your name), look into your Soul Urge, your Essence, and so on. You can decode your code, so to speak, by putting it all together in one big picture of your life. *Numerology for Your Home* by Amanda Rieger Green gives you a basic understanding of your personal environment, and how you can work with it, to tap into your own abundance codes.

Astrology and Numerology

Astrology and numerology combined provide a unique view on who you are and what you are experiencing. In combination, the astrological and numerological wisdom offered here help reveal the deeper story and panorama of your inner and outer life, creating the big picture of your life experience that is mind-blowingly accurate. The point in doing all of this is to obtain insight on your physical and spiritual worlds in creating ceremony for deepening your life—for creating a more abundant and enlightened YOU.

Ceremonies and Numerology

When looking at the Moon cycles for creating a ceremony, we can look at several factors to determine various numerology codes. We can calculate the numerology of the date, we can use the degree of the Moon sign, or we can work with the numbers of the time the ceremony occurs. Here are a few ways we like to incorporate numerology into our ceremonies:

1. **Calculating a date as a number to use in Ceremony.**

   Simply sum up the numbers of the entire date and reduce them to a single digit. For example, you decide to design a love magic ceremony on Valentine's Day. The date is 2/14/2020.

   The calculation:
   $2 + 1 + 4 + 2 + 0 + 2 + 0 = 11$

   $1 + 1 = 2$
   How perfect! Valentine's Day 2020 adds up to a 2, the number of partnership, balance, harmony and relationships. Bonus! The Master Number 11 shows up here in the calculation: 11 is the number of magic, making wishes come true, and transcendence. You can incorporate

numerology into this Valentines Love ceremony by setting some intentions using the energy of both 11 and 2.

2. **Incorporating the degree of the Zodiac as a number to use in Ceremony.**

Each of the twelve signs in the zodiac have thirty degrees. The New or Full Moon will be exact at a certain degree in a particular sign in the zodiac. Using your Wise Skies Digital Calendar or your preferred lunar calendar, you can identify the degree when the New or Full Moon becomes exact. You can use this degree as part of a greater number code within the ceremony.

For example, perhaps you want to design a House Blessing Ceremony on the New Moon in Cancer. The current New Moon is exact in 4 degrees of Cancer—perfect! The energy of the 4 will bring stability and order to the home you are blessing.

3. **Incorporating time as a number to use in Ceremony.**

You could also look at the time you wish to start the ceremony and use it as a number code.

For example:
You begin your ceremony at 4:08
$4 + 0 + 8 = 12$
$1 + 2 = 3$

Three is the number of "creation and communication." So, how can you use the magic of 3 in a ceremony? You could set 3 intentions around what you intend to create, including an intention for being authentic in your communication and using the power of your voice.

Let's put it all together in an example of how to use number codes in a New Moon Ceremony:

Date
July 12 (7+1+2) = 10
$(1 + 0) = 1$
1 = New Beginnings

Degree

20 Degrees (2 + 0) = 2

2 = Sincerity

Start Time

12:00 PM start time (1+2) = 3

3 = Creativity

You are working with a 1-2-3 code. You can weave the words and tones associated with 1-2-3 into your wishes, journal about them, and ask for insight and guidance around them.

Numerology Empowerment Codes

In this book, we have created a special Wise Skies code for you. We call it *New and Full Moon Numerology Empowerment Codes*. We use these codes as a way for you to be able to add a layer of energy, insight and relevance to your ceremonies. All of the work has been done for you in the following chapters. But we want to give you an explanation of how we have calculated this special code so you can work with it on your own if you choose.

We use the number associated with each astrological sign in its natural order. We assign Aries with the #1 because it is the first sign of the astrological calendar, Taurus is #2, and so forth.

Aries = 1	Libra = 7
Taurus = 2	Scorpio = 8
Gemini = 3	Sagittarius = 9
Cancer = 4	Capricorn = 10
Leo = 5	Aquarius = 11 Master Number
Virgo = 6	Pisces = 12

Don't worry! We have taken the numerology guesswork out so you can easily know which numbers to use, when, and why.

NEW MOON NUMEROLOGY EMPOWERMENT CODES

On each New Moon, the Sun and Moon are coupled together *or conjunct* in one sign. In other words, when the Sun and Moon are both in Aries, there is an Aries New Moon.

The New Moon Formula:
Let's use the Aries New Moon as an example.

Aries Numerology = 1
Sun + Moon both in Aries
Sun in Aries (1) + Moon in Aries (1) = 2

Aries New Moon Numerology Empowerment Code = 2
The Energy of 2 as calculated for use in an Aries New Moon ceremony promotes connection, balance and interdependence.

FULL MOON NUMEROLOGY EMPOWERMENT CODES

On each Full Moon, the Sun and the Moon are opposite each other, each one in a different sign.

Pay close attention as we will add together the number associated with the Sun sign and the number associated with the Moon sign for this intensely magical code. Why? We want to optimize the frequencies of both the Sun and the Moon along with the frequencies of their position in the zodiac.

The Full Moon Formula:
Let's continue using Aries as our example. During an Aries Full Moon, the Sun is in the sign *opposite* Aries, which is Libra.

Aries Numerology = 1 (where the Moon is during an Aries Full Moon)
Libra Numerology = 7 (where the Sun is during an Aries Full Moon)
Moon in Aries (1) + Sun in Libra (7) = 8

Aries Full Moon Numerology Empowerment Code = 8
The 8 energy encourages us to examine where we have a tendency to focus on external successes, our ego, and where we may be stubborn.

NUMEROLOGY CODE JOURNALING

In the ceremonies throughout this book, we offer journal prompts and thought-provoking questions associated with the numerological energy of each New

Moon and Full Moon. These questions are intended to offer extra insight and help you create a multi-dimensional ceremony.

For example: *Where does my ego block my fulfillment or sense of peace?*

Am I willing to let go of any ego-based fears in the energy of the Aries Full Moon in order to experience more abundance both spiritually and physically?

"The key to abundance is meeting limited circumstances with unlimited thoughts."

- Marianne Williamson, Author, Spiritual Leader, 2020 Democratic Presidential Candidate

PART 2

New Moon Ceremonies

Friendly reminder: If you're new to this, you may be thinking: "I'm an Aries!" and have fun identifying with some of the major Aries themes. However, we ALL live under the Aries New/Full Moon when it's high in the sky, and we can ALL take advantage of creating ceremony for an Aries Moon, no matter what our astrological birth sign. That is to say, the ceremonies in this book are not specific to your horoscope sign. They are specific to what is going on *in the Sky*.

Yes, you will need to know what sign the Moon is in to best use the ceremonies in this book. But you don't have to worry—there are free resources online to help you find what phase and sign the Moon is in. Once you know those two items, you're ready to use the ceremonies in this book.

New Moon Ceremonies

"The day that you plant the seed is not the day you eat the fruit."

- Fabienne Fredrickson

The New Moon is a lunar power time when your chakras—the energy centers in your body—are open and most receptive to starting something new, and to changing karmic patterns. The New Moon phase is an ideal time to receive divine blessings and insights for personal and spiritual growth. These lunar vibrations activate energy for finding practical solutions, reigniting passions, and taking the first step toward a new habit.

During the New Moon, we perform ceremonies to illuminate what we need to know about divine will in our life. We ask ourselves and God: What is the next right step? We can make wishes and set intentions not only for ourselves but also to raise the energy of the collective consciousness here on Earth.

Reminder: it takes time for wishes to manifest. The Universe is co-creating with you at it's own pace, weaving things together that are in your best interest, according to your unique needs and desires. Unanswered wishes are not mistakes.

New Moon Ceremony Suggestions

We offer ideas for ceremonies based on what we like to do, but the beauty of creating your own ceremony is that you get to intuitively make the rules. There is no right or wrong. Your motives, intentions, and humble connection to Spirit are what matter most.

We offer three core suggestions for your New Moon ceremonies:

(1) Conduct your ceremony and write wishes within the first eight hours of the New Moon - this is the most astrologically potent time to set intentions.

(2) Use at least one of the recommended tools from each of the elements listed below in step one, but you can use as many or as few as you like.

(3) Enjoy yourself - don't take things too seriously. These ceremonies are intended to be a fun way for you to co-create the life of your dreams, while honing your connection with the divine realm.

New Moon Invocation

New Moon invocations are dialogues or prayers with God or Spirit. Some of us view this as speaking directly to the personified energy of the New Moon and its innate intelligence, honoring it as a physical manifestation of God energy in this world. In whatever way you wish to view it, the invocation is a time of alignment with the divine force to ask for something new to be co-created.

Invocation also offers an opportunity to open and create sacred space. It is an invitation for the highest love and intelligence to be with you and support you throughout the ceremony.

Opening Sacred Space

Suggested for you to open sacred space for each New Moon ceremony.

Say: *I open this sacred space—calling in the highest love, light, and divine intelligence—and I align it with the purest energies of my mind, body, and spirit. I am a cosmic gardener, planting seeds with the highest and brightest frequencies to germinate and sprout in divine right timing.*

I trust the precision of universal flow. I honor those who came before me and those who will come after me. We are one.

Everything that is created is never destroyed, only transformed.

As above, so below.

I am a creator and transformer. May the New Moon in _____ (zodiac sign) open my heart to the newness of possibilities before me with grace, peace, and inspired vision. I invoke the highest energies of the _____ (zodiac sign) New Moon in love, in light, and in divine intelligence.

And so it is.

Closing Sacred Space

The below is our suggestion for you to close sacred space for each New Moon ceremony.

After the ceremony is complete, bring your palms together in front of your heart or your forehead (third eye). Close your eyes and take three breaths, breathing in and out through your nose.

Visualize a channel of white liquid light flowing through the crown of your head, down through your spine, and then down into the Earth to clear your physical, emotional, and spiritual body. Visualize this light becoming fluorescent in cleansing your DNA and the cells of your body, and then shining it's unique rays out from your heart into the world.

Say: *I honor myself, this sacred space, and the divine intelligence guiding my life. I trust my Higher Power to overlight my intentions and to align my heart with the highest good of the collective. This ceremony is whole and complete. I give thanks, it is done, and so it is. Namaste.*

With hands in prayer, bow to the inner divinity of your own sacred heart, honoring your highest self. Remember God with gratitude.

New Moon Ceremony in Spiritual India

Tiffany relates a personal story illustrating the power of a New Moon Ceremony.

Everyday is a ceremony in India, but this special trip in 2018, led by Claudia and Thomas of Del Sol Yoga and Kung Fu, culminated in an unforgettable New Moon Ceremony on the banks of the Ganges.

March 7, 2018: Mumbai

A man curls up in his seat beside me on the plane and snores. I admire people who can sleep in any condition, but he is taking up quite a bit of my personal space and I'm feeling squooshed. The Airplane dinner left something (all things) to be desired and my audiobook is now painting a grim picture of the child beggars in India. There is no respite for twenty hours. The flight is neither posh nor easy. But nothing is getting in the way of my excitement as we travel to Spiritual India.

We land in Mumbai. It's dark but the city is throbbing with honking horns, cattle in the road, and rickshaws swooping in and out between trucks. Smoky incense traces its way from the shops into the warm night Air. Our yogi bodies are geared to be awake and explore, but we are encouraged to rest: our USA day is India's night. After receiving a warm welcome with beautiful floral leis at the hotel, we retire to our rooms for a restless night.

March 8, 2018: Govardhan Ecovillage

Glass bowls of pink and white lotus flowers floating in Water are placed thoughtfully throughout the hotel cafe. Breakfast is the most amazing vegetarian buffet I've ever seen. I want to try everything: the flatbreads, the juices, the potatoes, the spicy chickpeas with spinach. We load our plates and sit by the pool where the plumeria are in their full glory. Men are smoking, tourists are taking pictures of the garden statues, and the birds have begun their morning songs. It's not long before we return our dishes, grab our bags, and board a bus.

There is nothing that can explain the chaotic rhythm of life on the roads in India. We see two dozen or more men standing like vertical sardines velcroed together in the back-back of large trucks. Women and children are riding side-saddle in surreal serenity behind motorcycle racers qualifying for the Paris-Dakar Rally. Rickshaws are darting in and out of it all at breakneck speed. Oddly, cattle, pigs, and monkeys walk the streets like Zen masters. They are one with the traffic. *Omm.* Nobody gets hit. Drivers swerve and honk as a kindness to the animals—not as an annoyance with fellow drivers.

Our teacher breaks out the harmonium for the first time. I'm in a bus full of yogis, floating through the traffic tetris, in the mecca of yogadom, chanting the names of the God with my friends and teachers. Put a fork in me.

It's hot, smoky, and holy. We are greeted with great kindness at the Govardhan ecovillage. Bhakti Yoga teacher and philosopher Radhanath Swami founded the ecovillage in 2003 as a spiritual retreat for people to be able to live in harmony with nature. We all read his book, *The Journey Home*, before coming. We admire his Seeker's heart and are eager to participate in some of his initiatives.

The schedule of the people living there is divine. Their day is an active ceremony. It's not one we are following on our short three days here, but it's one that appeals to our spiritual hearts.

We visit the rescue donkeys, who are wearing beaded necklaces, we tour the cattle barn where the calves are busy nursing, and we practice yoga in the studio above the barn, overlooking the mountains. It feels like home.

The sun is setting. It's time for Aarti, a daily ceremony and act of worship. The koi pond is hopping, an Indian guy is whisking around a large feathery looking object, and we are lighting little candles in tiny boats made of leaves and filled with flowers. Everyone is chanting again. We set our lights in the river when it's time. Prasad, a blessed dessert-like offering, is served in the same little leaf-bowls.

We walk back to one of the temples. The children are singing with great joy and great devotion. The little girls are on one side, and the boys are on the other. They are so happy to see our teacher that they grab him from our group and begin to dance with him.

A vegetarian meal is on its way. The food has been blessed and prepared with great reverence. It is served with great devotion. I make a mental note to check out the Hare Krishna cookbooks when we get back to Texas. I want to learn how to make some of this. Our teacher offers a lesson she will weave throughout the trip: Feed the people.

March 9, 2018: Ecovillage Gardening

It's India's morning. We didn't sleep much due to a relentless mosquito. We gather for yoga practice above the barn and eat breakfast together. The garden tour is the main activity of the day. We learn about their integrated Water conservation plan and how our flushing toilets are helping nurture the growth of the papayas. They teach us about their sustainability initiatives as well as gardening practices. I'm particularly curious about their pepper seeds and lemon grass.

March 10, 2018: Hiking the Mountains

We rise early again. The hike in the mountains is everything we wanted it to be. On the trail a group of locals pass us in an oxen-drawn carriage. A woman, an elder, stops and stares at us in awe. They are glad we are here. We are glad they are here. We can't communicate except through smiling eyes and hands in prayer position. She must have been three hundred years old.

March 11, 2018: The Road to Vrindavan

We leave in the darkness of the early morning. Tears are streaming down my face for many reasons, but mostly because I don't want to leave. Halfway through our drive, the harmonium is brought back out—the bus has a bad tire in the middle of nowhere India. There's no way we are going to make it to the Airport on time.

We broke down outside of the police station. Several of the yogis pile out of the bus to use their restroom, which is a hole in the ground. One of my friends shares her prophetic dream from the night before: we were running through the Airport and barely made our flight. Eventually the bus gets repaired and we careen through the Airport, getting on the plane in the nick of time.

The sun is setting and we are chanting in a bus once again as we arrive in the holy city of Vrindavan. We walk to the hotel, throw our bags in our rooms, and immediately run to the ISKCON temple (International Society for Krishna Consciousness) where a massive ceremony and celebration are going on. I get in semi-trouble for taking pictures of the ladies dancing: no cameras allowed. There are so many happy people. No matter where we go, there is a celebration every morning, and a celebration every night. Every town is vegetarian. I'm on a yogi-high.

Everyone respects each other with their hands in prayer and bowing from the heart. Each town has its own unique greeting. In Govardhan, it was "Hare Krishna" and here in Vrindavan it's "Radhe Radhe."

Back at the hotel, monkeys are peering at us through the windows in the cafe and they mean business. We've been warned: they will steal our sunglasses temporarily, until we make an offering of fruit, or fruit juice. Then, and only then, will the sunglasses be returned.

March 12, 2018: Sacred Temples of Vrindavan

We rise at 5:30am and filter enough Water for the morning. It's hard to breathe: there is an undeniable stench here that I can't get away from, not even in my room. The smells of open sewers, sweaty bodies, and the incense trying to cover it all up are overwhelming me. It's confusing to feel so dirty in a holy city.

The morning is busy with green birds, monkeys misbehaving, and a guy riding a camel by the money exchange store. We pass by a large group of Russians in the courtyard practicing yoga on our way to Ashtanga. We have a private room this morning. Yoga practice is a divine reminder to come back to the stillness of my own breath even when life is chaotic.

After breakfast, we pile in several rickshaws with some of the ISKCON guys who are helping guide us. They are taking us to the sacred sites today. Our first stop is a big red temple that is crawling with monkeys. Tears form in many of our eyes. We aren't sure why our hearts are stirred. "Vrindavan isn't like the rest of the world," our guide says. "You're on a spiritual plane here. Normal rules do not apply. Spiritual laws are governing you now."

I admit it feels a little like we have followed Alice down the rabbit hole. We walk through a huge festival back to our rickshaws. On the way to the next site we see sadhus, bodhi trees with crazy large root systems, and children playing with snakes. Cows are allowed to wander in the temples, and people are selling grass to feed the cows. It is said to be lucky to feed a cow your weight in grass while you are there.

We take a bus trip out to Govardhan Hill. It is considered a sacred site, a place where Krishna and his brother used to play, and a natural form of Krishna himself. It is said that Krishna lifted the hill for seven days to protect his people from the Rain God Indra.

Devotees are doing Parikramas (full body bows) 108 times in one spot before moving to the next spot as they make their way around the hill. It will take months to complete for those doing the full prostration (dandavata). Some carry milk and incense as an offering.

We have received a personal invitation to eat at the home of a friend of a friend thanks to our teachers. We sit on the floor and are served food as honored guests. Jet lag is kicking our ass and it's hard to stay awake. We lie on mats on the floor and are drifting off during the lessons and discussions.

We make our way back to Vrindavan. The sun sets over the Yamuna River, a tributary of the Ganges. We join the Aarti here and again light candles in little boats with flowers and put them in the river as a prayer.

As we leave, several children beg us for money, then put curses on us. They seem legit. We aren't sure how to handle this. We are here to help the children of Vrindavan, but not like this. The stench of the city is so bad we gag and puke in our scarves on the rickshaw ride back to the hotel.

March 13, 2018: Food For Life and Taj Mahal

It's a fasting day at the Food For Life school for girls. This means they only eat potatoes today. Our group is served potatoes on banana leaves, we sit on the floor. Pietor, the school's founder, sits down for breakfast with us and explains, "We don't need your millions of dollars, we need your pennies."

There is not a dry eye in our group when we leave breakfast for the morning assembly. Girls in blue uniforms sing their morning prayers and then rush to grab our hands so that we participate in the morning dancing. Smiles bigger than the whole country of India beam at us like prisms from the Sun.

The school has been educating and feeding impoverished girls in Vrindavan since 1991. A major aim of the school is to keep young girls in school through the age of eighteen to help them avoid arranged child marriage. We listen to their horror stories and their stories of triumph. We learn about the young girl who recently shaved her head to thwart a child marriage—and it worked. We hear about the girl who thinks she will only ever carry bricks on her head for a living to support her family, and how she now wants to be a pilot.

We visit the bull pen, where they keep the bulls that pull the carts that pick up the girls every morning. Even these bulls are a rescue mission. Once discarded and roaming the streets hungry, the bulls now have a job as school bus drivers. We tour the school: the library, the music room, and the craft room with looms for weaving.

We are simultaneously reduced and expanded by being here. It feels wrong to leave the school. We pledge our commitment to sponsor at least one girl each from three years old to eighteen. These are the front lines that, after walking them, you are forever changed.

In contrast, we now leave for a day trip to Agra to see the Taj Mahal. It feels like a long ride as we sit with mixed emotions. Originally commissioned in 1632 as a tomb, the Taj was completed in 1653. The cost of building is estimated at $827 million dollars. Despite the beauty of the marble building inlaid with precious stones, I can't help but think about the hungry mouths that $827 million could feed.

We have been from the lowest of lows to the highest of highs all within one day. A lot of questions come with that. I sit as close to the ISKCON guide as I can on the bus ride to pick his brain and soak up his responses.

March 14, 2018: Rishikesh

This morning we drive to Rishikesh, haven of yogis at the foothills of the Himalayas. There is a massive Shiva statue in the hotel overlooking the Ganges that is warm and inviting. We drop our bags in our rooms and meet again in the lobby. We drink chai, wander through a music store, and eventually cross over the tiny bridge into the other side of the city. At dinner, there is a sultan with an intimidating sword eating with some hippies. All are welcome here.

March 15, 2018: Day of the Dead

March 15th is our new day of the dead. Several in our group have an out of body experience as we pivot from beds to toilets all night and all day. Thankfully the doctor traveling with us is able to easily purchase shots and medication. It wouldn't be until months later that we found out it was shigella. For now, we suffer, knowing we are missing out on India, knowing this is part of the experience, knowing we are right where we are supposed to be.

March 16, 2018: Beatles Ashram & Ramana's Garden

We aren't well, but we march on. One foot in front of the other we make it to the Beatles ashram, which is located within an elephant and tiger sanctuary. We take turns taking pictures in the various stone meditation huts. This is where Maharishi Mahesh Yogi taught transcendental meditation in the 1960's and 1970's. I can't take another step and decide to lay down by a tree while the others continue. If I die here, let it be epic.

An hour later, the group returns and we walk together for Aarti on the banks of the Ganges. I'm not well. But I'm not missing this. There is marijuana growing freely on the side of the road with leaves larger than basketballs. There are beautiful murals of gurus along cement walls in the alleys. Street cats circle us for attention.

There is a large statue of Hanuman, the monkey-god devoted to Lord Rama. The monkey is holding his heart wide open so that all can see Rama and Sita are in his heart. We are bhakti yogis. We are reminded to find devotion in our hearts.

People are hungry, but I'm not sure how. I'm not quite able to eat yet. Regardless, dinner is at the organic cafe within Ramana's Garden, a children's home on the banks of the Ganges. Ramana's Garden provides education and housing for children who live below the poverty line or who have been victims of abuse. Organic gardening and cooking are part of the education. A couple is playing the guitar and singing devotional songs while the children are lighting candles on our table. After dinner, the community sits down for kirtan, a group call and response singing.

March 17, 2018: New Moon in Pisces

This morning I'm feeling like I have my life back. Health is returning. We do some whiteWater rafting in the Ganges then take a jeep ride into the Himalayas. Our next adventure is hiking several hours up to Shiva's cave.

Who is Shiva, you ask? He's one of the main Gods in Shaivism (a form of Hinduisim). And before you ask, no, I don't worship multiple gods—there's just the one that I know of, that has many faces. Shiva is the form of God that acts as destroyer, creator, and transformer. He is known as the patron of yoga and meditation, protector of yogis. He is often depicted carrying a trident, or with a trident on his third eye.

At the base of the hike, a local guide draws a trident in ashes on our foreheads. Today the New Moon is in Pisces, ruled by the planet Neptune. Is it a coincidence that in Greek mythology Neptune, God of the Sea, also carries a trident? We find a stick shaped like a trident on our way to the top.

In the cave, a six-foot tall sadhu unwraps his turban, allowing his dreadlocks to hang loose. They extend the length of his body and drag on the floor behind him like a bridal veil. We arrive in perfect timing for the Sun to blaze a stream of light through a crack in the cave's ceiling. It reminds me of being in the ancient Incan city of Machu Picchu when the Sun lights the heart of the Andes in Peru. Something deep, holy, and mysterious is going on in the cave as we sit down for meditation.

After the hike, I bought a shiva trident to commemorate the day. It seemed like a good idea at the time, but would give me hell at every Airport from Bombay to Austin.

We return to the hotel to shower and prepare for the New Moon ceremony: a Fire puja on the banks of the Ganges. A Brahmin priest is preparing a Fire. We circle around him and he begins to pass bowls of different herbs that we will be placing as blessings into the Fire.

Fire pujas are ceremonies that offer purification on the path toward enlightenment. Once a year, the New Moon in Pisces offers a unique window of time to set intentions around all things Piscean, including yoga and meditation practices. The whole trip has prepared us for this moment, to embrace the dark and the light, to purify and cleanse, to walk in truth, and to incorporate the sacred in our daily lives.

There is a tiny death that happens in the Dark Moon just before the New Moon is exact. The sun has set. We close our eyes, but the flicker of the Fire remains present.

My New Moon in Pisces Intention feels small, simple, profound, and powerful: "I connect with the Divine in my own heart with renewed commitment to the daily discipline of yoga and meditation." A new seed has been planted. My time in Spiritual India has come to a close. Namaste.

Looking back

It takes time for wishes to manifest. The Universe co-creates with us at its own pace, weaving things together that are in our best interest, according to our unique needs and desires. We can plant the seed, but we must wait on divine right timing for the harvest.

A wish set in motion on the banks of the Ganges under the Pisces New Moon was granted, in divine right timing . . . and in a way I never saw coming.

A year and a half after the trip to India, I completed yoga teacher training and now offer yoga and meditation classes as an extension of my personal practice. Teaching classes is a commitment that helps me stay the course with my daily disciplines while sharing the wisdom of the yogis—even better than I had wished.

Aries New Moon

WHEN THE NEW MOON IS IN ARIES

When the New Moon falls in the Fire sign of Aries, you can expect some sparks to fly. You might notice extra energy, including some sassy and spirited vibes. This is the perfect Moon to initiate a new project, to set an intention around new habits, or to start something new. This is the Moon of the pioneer and the spiritual warrior. It's time to bang the drum of self-confidence and look at the world with fresh eyes.

Aries is the first sign in the zodiac and is represented by the Ram. It is a Fire sign, ruled by the planet Mars.

Positive (High) Vibes of the Aries New Moon

(*Make wishes in these areas*)

Starting something new: hobbies, habits, and health routines
Drive and high energy
Pioneering spirit
Paving the way for new beginnings
Individuality
Boldness
Mental wellness
Personal responsibility
Assertiveness and confidence
Authentic and genuine communication

Challenging (Low) Vibes of the Aries New Moon

(*What you might wish to remove*)

Know-it-all attitudes
Bossy-ness
Short temper
Defensiveness
Dealing with enemies

Antagonistic attitudes
Conflicts
Self-centered viewpoint

In Health, Aries Governs

(Areas of the body where you might wish for healing)

Head
Spinal cord
Face
Brain
Complexion
Solar Plexus Chakra (Manipura Chakra)

Sample Wishes for the New Moon in Aries

- I easily find my self initiating healthy eating habits.
- I'm comfortable finding my independence in XYZ situation.
- I embrace a total healing in the area of my head and face.
- I connect with my potential through patience and awareness.

Aries New Moon Intention

I desire willingness to take right action organically and to welcome new opportunities in divine right timing. I am full of joy and ease.

Aries New Moon Healing Invocation

I invoke sacred healing space and experience a complete and total healing in my head, face, and solar plexus. My brain is functioning at optimum potential. I trust that I am wholly supported in the healing process.

Word to the Wise

When the Moon is in Aries, you are likely feeling hot, possibly irritable, and ready for action. Depending on your personal constituency and situation, you may enjoy the Fire energy. But if things are feeling too heated, you can incorporate elements from the opposite sign throughout the day to balance things out. The opposite sign of Aries is the Air sign Libra. Consider contemplative activities such as a walking meditation in a labyrinth to combine action (Fire) with mindfulness (Air). Combining Air and Fire elements assists you in transmuting your intentions into the highest and brightest frequencies.

Working with Corresponding Elements

We suggest using one or more items of your choice from each element when designing your ceremony. Use as many or as few as you like.

ARIES **Fire** items: Candles + Smoke

- Red and pink candles - love
- Spicy scented candles, herbal bundles, or incense:
    - Frankincense - holiness
    - Clove - purification
    - Cinnamon - abundance

ARIES **Earth** items: Crystals + Stones

- Bloodstone - protection
- Shungite - groundedness
- Agate - balancing
- Red Jasper - spiritual grounding

ARIES **Air** items: Intentions + Mantras

- Any personal wishes you want to make in the areas Aries governs + the High Vibe Aspects of Aries
- Aries New Moon Intention
- Aries New Moon Healing Invocation

ARIES **Water** items: Essential Oils + Flower Essences

- Myrrh - restorative
- Cedar - cleansing
- Spruce - grounding
- Ylang Ylang - harmonizing
- Geranium - uplifting

ARIES NEW MOON NUMEROLOGY

There are many ways to incorporate numerology when formulating your ceremony. You can find numbers to work with in the degree of the sign, the date, the hour you conduct the ceremony, etc. The New Moon Numerology Empowerment Code is a special formula developed by Amanda Rieger Green, MPH at Wise Skies. We like to think of this as part of our secret sauce. We use this number to find synchronicities as well as journaling on the day of the New Moon.

Aries New Moon Numerology Empowerment Code = 2

Numbers have power. We add the numbers that correlate with the Sun sign and the Moon sign, to create a unique code to use in ceremonies. During the New Moon, the Sun and the Moon appear in the same zodiac sign. That means each one is assigned the same number as the zodiac sign of Aries.

The Wise Skies Aries Formula:
Aries Numerology Code = 1
Sun in Aries (1) + Moon in Aries (1) = 2

The "2" Empowerment Code promotes connection, balance, and interdependence.

Notice when you see a 2 today: it's a reminder to stay connected. The 2 is also the frequency of relationships and harmony. Seeing a 2 reminds you to pause and find a healthy balance. It can enhance your ceremony to incorporate 2 of anything in your design.

Numerology Code Journaling

- *What does balanced connection feel like to me?*
- *How can I incorporate an interdependent attitude into all of my relationships and partnerships?*

ARIES NEW MOON CEREMONY
Moving Forward with Clarity

The ceremony for the New Moon in Aries helps you cultivate your super powers of intention and visualization. This ceremony is ideal for starting something new, gaining clarity, and sharpening the focus of your goals and dreams. If you feel like you've been sending mixed messages to the Universe, this ceremony is ideal to reset and recenter.

BEFORE YOU BEGIN GATHERING TOOLS, SAY THE NEW MOON INVOCATION FOUND ON PAGE XX.

Step One: Selecting Tools

Set up a New Moon wishing area in a quiet space without distractions. Ideally you can do this outdoors, but a private space inside works too. Refer to the corresponding elements in the section above to select your tools. We suggest incorporating at least one tool per element (Fire, Earth, Air, Water), as well as a journal to write your intentions and responses to the journal prompts.

Step Two: Fire it Up

Light a candle or incense. Close your eyes and slowly inhale the aromatic fragrance, exhaling slowly. Slow the breath down in order to become centered and grounded. Begin to feel connected to your body, mind, and spirit. Open your eyes and gaze into the flame. Inhale and exhale deeply three or four times. When you feel centered and focused, open the ceremony.

Say: *I am clear. I am centered. I am empowered through my eternal flame of being.*

Step Three: Oils & Crystals

Dab a few drops of essential oil(s) on your belly above the naval (Solar Plexus), between the eyes (Third Eye), and on the back of your neck (Throat Chakra). Inhale and exhale deeply three times.

The left side of the body is the receptive side of the body, and draws energy to you. Place the crystals you've chosen to work with in your left hand with a few drops of essential oils. Inhale and exhale deeply to continue clearing and purifying your energy.

Step Four: Meditate

Continue to gaze into the soft light of a candle in meditation (five to twenty minutes). Without concentrating on anything in particular, this meditative state allows you to soften and become more receptive to the energies and intentions you want to welcome. This time also prepares your heart-space to become aware of whatever is blocking you, or to address what needs to be healed in order to move forward. Spiritual nod: The intentional letting go of personal aims and wounds opens space for God or Spirit to create something beautiful and new its place.

Step Five: Connect

Now, connect with your heart and ask your Higher Self what you need to know in the current moment.

Say: *What tools, information and resources will best aid me in my journey throughout the month and the astrological year?*

Listen for response. Write it down in your journal. Anything that occurs to you in this moment is your intuition. Even if an answer doesn't make sense now, go ahead and write it down so that you can reflect on these insights as the month unfolds.

Step Six: Divine Support

Ask your cosmic helpers to assist you in manifesting your New Moon wishes, knowing that you are being supported by a collective wisdom far greater than your own ideas. You will want to reach out in prayer to Spirit, Higher Self, God, the Universe, spirit helpers, your guardians and ancestors, angels, etc.

Say: *Spirit of the Universe, please set aside what I think I want so that my desires are in alignment with my soul's purpose and highest calling.*

Spirit of the Fire, please clarify my wishes and intentions.

Spirit of the Earth, please receive what is in line with my soul's purpose at this time.

Step Seven: Set Intentions

Pull inspiration and insights from your meditation, the New Moon numerology, and the properties of Aries (as listed above in the areas Aries governs + the High Vibe Aspects of Aries) to write up to ten intentions in your journal. This is also an ideal time to write the New Moon Intention and the Healing Invocation. The most potent time for wish-making is within eight hours of the New Moon. Reminder: in this instance, the Aries energy supports you in activating something new.

To activate your intention, take a small piece of paper and write down key words from one main wish—the thing that you most feel called to begin.

Softly blow into the Fire of the candle flame or into the smoke of the incense. Affirm that any unwanted energy is now clearing out with your breath. You are not blowing the candle out, you are simply mixing the Fire with your breath to purify and cleanse.

Use the Fire or smoke to transmute your main wish into the ethers. You can carefully burn the piece of paper, or you can wave the paper in the smoke without lighting it at all. As a third option, you can simply say the key words of your wish out loud while focusing on the Fire, then bury your paper in your garden or a special spot outside.

Sending your main intention into the Fire or smoke is a form of creating energetic or spiritual alchemy—the ancient practice of transforming something into a higher vibrational frequency.

Step Eight: Visualize

Sit again with your eyes closed. Visualize your main wish coming to fruition. How will it look when the intentions and wishes unfold? How will you feel? Where is it taking place? Be willing to have faith, and believe that your cosmic guidance team is supporting you in what is best for you at this time.

Say: *Thank you, Fire (extinguish your Fire and give a spiritual nod to the Earth, Wind, and Water elements, adding your own thoughts of gratitude).*

Step Nine: Crystal Magic

Set the crystals on top of your journal in the darkness of the New Moon for three nights. This allows the crystals to recharge their energy and to support your intentions. If you cannot leave the crystals and journal outside, you can put them in a window sill.

After three nights, retrieve the crystals with gratitude. Keep them in your pocket, next to your bed, in your car, or somewhere close by over the next few weeks. Did you know some people talk to their plants and crystals? If you want to play in this realm, you can silently thank the crystals, acknowledging them for their support and intelligence.

Option: Discipline and routine is the key. Commit to opening your journal every morning for the next two weeks. With the same crystals in your left hand, read your New Moon intentions out loud. You can also use the essential oils you used in the ceremony. This not only engages your muscle memory, it beams a signal to the Universe that you are purposefully aligning your energy with your intentions with great commitment. You can even relight your candle or incense during this time. Make it your own morning ritual for the next two weeks and see what unfolds.

Step Ten: Closing Sacred Space

It is important to seal the energy after any ceremony. Refer to **page xx** for our suggestion on closing sacred space, or say your personalized closing prayers.

MAKING IT PERSONAL

Moon Musings
- Amanda

The New Moon in Aries is my astrological opposite and half birthday because my Sun is in Libra. I love this New Moon energy to "balance" out my indecisive or people pleasing, low vibing Libra energies. I usually set intentions about individuality, bold action and channeling my Aries medicine. Here are a few of my Moon musings from past Aries New Moons:

- I use my independent voice with peace and ease. I speak my truth, even in the face of adversity or tension.
- I create sustainable energy and forward momentum for all projects, endeavors, and undertakings, trusting others to help me along the way.

- My goals of writing my first book are comfortably within my reach. I consistently create time to write and trust the universe to weave a web of support around me like magic.
- Over the course of the next six months, I eagerly initiate new projects that help me cultivate an abundant lifestyle, working and living anywhere in the world.
- I am the highest light, love and expression of myself in all aspects of my life.

Best Wishes

- Tiffany

The New Moon in Aries hits in my 4th or 5th house depending on the degree of the New Moon. So, sometimes I add elements relating to home and family (4th house) or love-given (5th house) issues. Here are a few wishes I have used on previous Aries New Moons:

- I easily begin a writing routine that is fun and results in completing my bestselling novel and netflix series.
- I welcome vitality into my body, clarity into my mind, and peace into my soul by living my best life.
- I embrace loving myself with confidence by living well in my temple.
- I easily initiate connection with my important relationships in ways that create mutual trust, love, support, and understanding.
- I am easily cultivating an off-grid lifestyle full of natural wonder, healthy gardening, and simple joys.
- Above all, help me set aside what I think I know, and what I think I want, so that the Divine can flow through me. May I be of service to God and my fellows.

Taurus New Moon

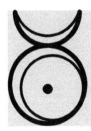

WHEN THE NEW MOON IS IN TAURUS

When the New Moon falls in the Earth sign of Taurus, you can expect to feel easy-going, affectionate, and persistent. You might also notice yourself or others becoming more obstinate. This is the perfect Moon to set intentions around stability, predictability, and any area where you are seeking a sense of rootedness. This is the Moon of promises, creature comforts, and values. It's time to bang the drum of self-worth and perhaps offer a renewed sense of commitment to some area of your life.

Taurus is the second sign in the zodiac and is represented by the Bull. It is an Earth sign, ruled by the planet Venus.

Positive (High) Vibes of the Taurus New Moon

(*Make wishes in these areas*)

Consistency and patience
Loyalty
Nurturing through food
Self-worth
Core values and manners
Money and wealth-building
Sensuality and pleasure
Security and stability through slow and steady growth
Combining the old and the new: think vintage charm
Perseverance and contentment

Challenging (Low) Vibes of the Taurus New Moon

(*What you might wish to remove*)

Stubbornness
Laziness
Slow to change or make decisions
Tire-kicking

Overly protective or territorial
Possessiveness
Attachment
Stagnation

In Health, Taurus Governs

(Areas of the body where you might wish for healing)

Throat and neck
Coughs
Speech and vocal cords
Thyroid
Throat Chakra (Vishudha Chakra)
Root Chakra (Muladhara Chakra)

Sample Wishes for the New Moon in Taurus

- I easily find myself taking right action towards home ownership.
- I embrace an attitude of patience and perseverance.
- I am led to the right team who can help with a complete and total healing of my throat and thyroid.

Taurus New Moon Intention

I feel safe and secure in my own skin, trusting that all experiences, no matter how challenging, are lessons to expand my horizons and motivate my personal evolution.

Taurus New Moon Healing Invocation

I invoke sacred healing space with clear speech, impeccable words, both spoken and unspoken, activating the intelligence of the universe within my DNA and cells. My throat, neck, vocal cords, and thyroid function at optimal health through the ceremonial process and beyond.

Word to the Wise

When the Moon is in Taurus, you are likely feeling connected and grounded. Depending on your personal constituency and situation, you may enjoy the security and stability the Earth energy provides. But if things are feeling dense, fixed, or even stuck, you can incorporate elements from the opposite sign throughout the day to balance things out. The opposite sign of Taurus is the Water sign Scorpio. Consider Water-related activities to encourage fluidity: taking baths, drinking tea, making spritzes, using herbal sprays and tinctures, swimming in hot springs or a lake. It can be useful to combine the steadfastness of your intentions (Earth) with the flexibility of trusting providence to flow in at divine right timing (Water).

Working with Corresponding Elements

We suggest using one or more items of your choice from each element when designing your ceremony. Use as many or as few as you like.

TAURUS **Fire** items: Candles + Smoke

- Green, brown, and tan candles - nature + nurture
- Woodsy scented candles, herbal bundles, or incense:
  - Sage - clearing
  - Cedar - grounding
  - Rosemary - passion

TAURUS **Earth** items: Crystals + Stones

- Tiger's Eye - empowerment
- Rose Quartz -compassion
- Red Jasper - trust
- Malachite - energetic clearing
- Sodalite - authentic communication
- Rutilated Quartz - spiritual development

TAURUS **Air** items: Intentions + Mantras

- Any personal wishes you want to make in the areas Taurus governs + the High Vibe Aspects of Taurus
- Taurus New Moon Intention
- Taurus New Moon Healing Invocation

TAURUS **Water** items: Essential Oils + Flower Essences

- Vetiver - spiritual grounding
- Clary Sage - protection
- Rose - love
- Bergamot - eliminating fear

TAURUS NEW MOON NUMEROLOGY

There are many ways to incorporate numerology when formulating your ceremony. You can find numbers to work with in the degree of the sign, the date, the hour you conduct the ceremony, etc. The New Moon Numerology Empowerment Code is a special formula developed by Amanda Rieger Green, MPH at Wise Skies. We like to think of this as part of our secret sauce. We use this number to find synchronicities as well as journaling on the day of the New Moon.

Taurus New Moon Numerology Empowerment Code = 4

Numbers have power. We add the numbers that correlate with the Sun sign and the Moon sign, to create a unique code to use in ceremonies. During the New Moon, the Sun and the Moon appear in the same zodiac sign. That means each one is assigned the same number as the zodiac sign of Taurus.

The Wise Skies Formula:
Taurus Numerology Code = 2
Sun in Taurus (2) + Moon in Taurus (2) = 4

The "4" Empowerment Code promotes stability, process, and organization. Notice when you see a 4 today—it's a reminder to get grounded. Seeing a 4 reminds you to pause and determine an order of operations: what needs to be done next? It can enhance your ceremony to incorporate 4 of anything in your design.

Numerology Code Journaling

- *When do I experience stability?*
- *What does stability feel like to me?*
- *How can I organize myself during the Taurus New Moon to promote optimal outcomes in all aspects of my life?*

TAURUS NEW MOON CEREMONY
Root to Rise

This ceremony is ideal for setting intentions that stimulate financial flow, as well as invoke security, connection, and a sense of groundedness. Like the plant world, we must first feel deeply rooted, before we can advance and grow. You will bury your intentions, crystals, and other elements for 6 months as your intentions solidify in Mother Earth.

BEFORE YOU BEGIN GATHERING TOOLS, SAY THE NEW MOON INVOCATION FOUND ON PAGE XX.

Step One: Selecting Tools

Set up a New Moon wishing area in a quiet space without distractions. Ideally you can do this outdoors, but a private space inside works too. Refer to the corresponding elements in the section above to select your tools. We suggest incorporating at least one tool per element (Fire, Earth, Air, Water), as well as a journal to write your intentions and responses to the journal prompts. For this ceremony, we also recommend a chai tea and some meditation music.

Step Two: Tea Time

Brew a cup of your favorite tea. We like Tumeric or Chai for the Taurus New Moon. Add almond milk and agave as needed, and use your favorite mug to make it extra nurturing. Drink the tea and begin to relax, settling into the magic of the New Moon and your own presence.

Step Three: Reflection Vibes

Read and re-read the Taurus intention and Taurus healing invocation in the section above to ignite the Taurean energy. Light your candle/incense or dried herb bundle, and play some soothing meditation music. Place the crystals you're working with around you in a grid, or hold them in your palms. Meditate on the Taurus intention for five to ten minutes.

Step Four: Intentions + Earth

Write up to ten intentions and/or wishes on a piece of paper that you can bury. Reminder: To harness the power of the New Moon, it's important to write your wishes within eight hours after the exact time of the New Moon (please do not write wishes before). Refer to our sample wishes above for guidance.

Choose a place to bury the paper where you have written your intentions. If you don't have access to a place to bury them in the ground, you can get creative by hiding them under the couch cushion.

Say: *Take these intentions and let their highest essence germinate in the darkness to invoke the best possible outcome in the light.*

Options: Bury the crystals with your intentions and dig them up on the Taurus Full Moon in approximately six months. Or, you can simply place the crystals on top of the burial spot for three days and three nights.

When you unEarth the intentions, you have several options to transmute the energy further. You can place the intentions with the crystals and some of the dirt from the burial spot into ice trays to freeze them. The intention-ice-cubes can be dropped into a bath, spread in your yard, or offered to a plant.

Step Five: Seal the Deal

Dab a few drops of essential oils on the front and back of your neck and behind your ears (being mindful not to get the oil around your eyes). Sit down next to your sacred burial spot and meditate for 4 minutes (the Taurus New Moon numerology code of stability to ground your wishes). Conjure the feeling of having each of your intentions fulfilled.

Step Six: Closing Sacred Space

It is important to seal the energy after any ceremony. Refer to **page xx** for our suggestion on closing sacred space, or say your personalized closing prayers.

MAKING IT PERSONAL

Moon Musings
- Amanda

I always tell people I want to come back as a Taurus Sun in my next life. Why? I have a Scorpio - Taurus interception in my natal astrological chart and my Chiron is in Taurus. During Taurus New Moons, I usually do ceremonies outside with crystals, my oracle deck, and intentions on Moon paper charged from the Taurus Full Moon. Here are a few musings from previous Taurus New Moons:

- I believe that I am always in the right place at the right time and experiences unfold more abundantly than I can possibly imagine.
- I am secure in my heart, body, mind, and spirit, knowing that I am supported and secure in all aspects of my life. I am safe.
- The words I speak to myself, to others, and to the universe are of integrity, impeccable character, and abundance. I organically communicate with genuine truth in all interactions.
- I plant seeds for financial security, prosperity, and support that unfold over the next month and 6 months in divine timing. I am generous with my abundance.
- I heal wounds of insecurity, lack-consciousness, and fear-based beliefs with rigorous honesty, healthy vulnerability, and trust. I am healing.

Best Wishes
- Tiffany

The New Moon in Taurus hits my 5th or 6th house depending on the degree of the New Moon. So, sometimes I add elements relating to love-given (5th house) or health issues (6th house). Here are a few wishes I have used on previous Taurus New Moons:

- I gain clarity in thinking regarding budgeting, spending, and saving money, leading to my ability to handle resources wisely as a good steward of finances.
- Money flows to and through me in a happy way that provides joy, stability, and security.

- I easily find myself taking steps that lead to owning my own homestead with breathtaking views, in a like-minded community, at a price I can afford.
- I find myself joyfully, consistently, and consciously counting my blessings and appreciating nature with childlike wonder.
- I experience satisfaction in all areas of my life at the end of each day.
- Above all, help me set aside what I think I know, and what I think I want, so that the Divine can flow through me. May I be of service to God and my fellows.

Gemini New Moon

WHEN THE NEW MOON IS IN GEMINI

When the New Moon falls in the Air sign of Gemini, you can expect plans to change. You might notice a need to be around friends, be social, and to keep a lot of tabs open on your computer. You might also sense a need to communicate ideas. This is the perfect Moon to talk it out, send a newsletter, start a writing group, or launch a book. This is the Moon of the multi-tasker, the social butterfly, and the curious Seeker. It is time to bang the drum of self-inquisition and approach the world with a fresh perspective: we're all crewmates on the same boat.

Gemini is the third sign in the zodiac and is represented by the Twins. It is an Air sign, ruled by the planet Mercury.

Positive (High) Vibes of the Gemini New Moon

(*Make wishes in these areas*)

Multi-tasking
Focus and attention to detail
Writing, editing, speaking, and reading
Clear communication and healthy discussions
Mental stimulation
Intelligence, intellect and quick wit
Mindfulness and being present
Micro goals
Social opportunities
Work with hands: handyman, typing, knitting, playing instruments, etc.

Challenging (Low) Vibes of the Gemini New Moon

(*What you might wish to remove*)

Overcommitment
Overthinking
Detachment

Indecision
Impulsivity
Anxieties

In Health, Gemini Governs

Lungs and breathing
Shoulders and collar bone
Arms, wrists, and hands
Nervous system
Throat Chakra (Vishuddha Chakra)
Third Eye (Anja Chakra)

Sample Wishes for the New Moon in Gemini

- I commit to writing one newsletter (or chapter of my book) per month.
- I enjoy connecting with friends through social activities.
- I easily find myself reading one new book per month.

Gemini New Moon Intention

I trust divine right timing and willingly communicate with integrity, transparency, and consistency. My inside voice matches my outside voice.

Gemini New Moon Healing Invocation

I invoke sacred healing space with clarity of breath throughout my chest, shoulders, collar bone, arms, wrists, and hands, oxygenating my entire being with the breath of life, love, and divine flow. My mind, body, and spirit emanate a calming, healing presence.

Word to the Wise

When the Moon is in Gemini, it's possible you are feeling pulled in many directions. Depending on your personal constituency and situation, you may enjoy the endless options provided under an Air-Moon. But if things are feeling too indecisive and scattered, you can incorporate elements from the opposite sign throughout the day to balance things out. The opposite sign of Gemini is Sagittarius. Consider contemplative yoga or something that combines thought (Air) with action (Fire).

Working with Corresponding Elements

We suggest using one or more items of your choice from each element when designing your ceremony. Use as many or as few as you like.

GEMINI **Fire** items: Candles + Smoke

- Blue and yellow candles - stimulating
- Uplifting citrus and herbal scented candles, herbal bundles, or incense:
    - Lavender - calming
    - Sage - clearing
    - Orange - uplifting

GEMINI **Earth** items: Crystals + Stones

- Labradorite - magic
- Aquamarine - letting go
- Blue or Green Kyanite - alignment
- Rainbow Obsidian - auric grounding
- Apache Tear - energetic clarity

GEMINI **Air** items: Intentions + Mantras

- Any personal wishes you want to make in the areas Gemini governs + the High Vibe Aspects of Gemini
- Gemini New Moon Intention
- Gemini New Moon Healing Invocation

GEMINI **Water** items: Essential Oils + Flower Essences

- Basil - blessings
- Neroli - sensual comfort
- Orange - cheerful
- Lemon - zest
- Citrus - uplifting
- Grapefruit - spiritual clearing
- Pennyroyal - peacekeeping

GEMINI NEW MOON NUMEROLOGY

There are many ways to incorporate numerology when formulating your ceremony. You can find numbers to work with in the degree of the sign, the date, the hour you conduct the ceremony, etc. The New Moon Numerology Empowerment Code is a special formula developed by Amanda Rieger Green,

MPH at Wise Skies. We like to think of this as part of our secret sauce. We use this number to find synchronicities as well as journaling on the day of the New Moon.

Gemini New Moon Numerology Empowerment Code = 6

Numbers have power. We add the numbers that correlate with the Sun sign and the Moon sign to create a unique code to use in ceremonies. During the New Moon, the Sun and the Moon appear in the same zodiac sign. That means each one is assigned the same number as the zodiac sign of Gemini.

The Wise Skies Formula:
Gemini Numerology Code = 3
Sun in Gemini (3) + Moon in Gemini (3) = 6

The "6" Empowerment Code promotes compassion, healing, and intuition.

Notice when you see a 6 today: it's a reminder to be compassionate. Seek to understand where other people are coming from with patience and tolerance when you see a 6. It can enhance your ceremony to incorporate 6 of anything in your design.

Numerology Code Journaling

- *When do I actively practice giving and receiving compassion in my life?*
- *What healing is necessary in this Gemini New Moon energy for me to experience more peace and more clearly tap into my intuition?*

GEMINI NEW MOON CEREMONY

Connection through Communication

We use cacao and divination to activate our throat chakras under the Gemini New Moon. This ceremony is ideal for strengthening clear communication and gaining discernment.

BEFORE YOU BEGIN GATHERING TOOLS, SAY THE NEW MOON INVOCATION FOUND ON PAGE XX.

Step One: Selecting Tools

Set up a New Moon wishing area in a quiet space without distractions. Ideally you can do this outdoors, but a private space inside works too. Refer to the corresponding elements in the section above to select your tools. We suggest incorporating at least one tool per element (Fire, Earth, Air, Water), as well as a journal to write your intentions and responses to the journal prompts. You'll also need a tarot or oracle deck as well as some cacao tea. Both can be ordered online.

Step Two: Clear the Energy

Start by taking a cleansing breath of one of your essential oils, then exhale and pause. Count backwards: 3, 2, 1. Breathe in and relax. Dab a few drops of the essential oil on the back of your neck, throat, behind your ears, and along your spine for extra grounding and clarity (be careful, some essential oils can sting).

Say: *I am rooted. I am grounded. My energy field is safe, sustainable, and sacred.*

Step Three: Blend in

Cacao teas are made with cacao nibs that are brewed and infused like loose leaf tea. Brew some cacao tea, or for a treat, you can also create a blend of cacao powder and milk (coconut or almond). Our ritual cacao drink recipe is below.

Drink the tea and begin to shuffle a tarot deck or oracle deck that you love. The deck can be new to you, or one you have used for several years. Ask for expanded consciousness and for insight to flow naturally while shuffling.

Step Four: Messages from the Universe

Knock on the deck to clear it, then shuffle the cards a few more times. Ask yourself "what do I need to know right now, during this New Moon?" Pull one card (or more if you need further clarification). Read the meaning of the card you pulled and see how it resonates with your current situation. Journal any insights or aha moments you receive from the magical tarot messages.

Step Five: Writing Wishes

Pull inspiration and insights from your card meditation and the properties of Gemini (as listed above in the sample wishes, the areas Gemini governs + the High Vibe Aspects of Gemini) to write up to ten intentions in your journal. This is also an ideal time to write the New Moon Intention and the Healing Invocation. The most potent time for wish-making is within eight hours of the New Moon.

Step Six: Into the Darkness

In the evening, once you have spent time journaling about your personal reading and written your wishes, place your journal, deck of cards, crystals, and candle(s) or herb bundle under the darkness of the Gemini New Moon. If the weather is inclement, you can place your sacred ceremony items next to a window or similar space shielded from the elements. Leave them to germinate in the darkness for three days and nights. Remember that your ceremony is still open and active during this time.

After the three days, gather your ceremony items. Brew another cup of cacao tea. Ask once more for further intelligence and guidance. Knock once on the deck to clear it, then shuffle the deck several times.

Say: *Please send me further clarity, instruction, and divine intelligence to propel me forward in the darkness of the New Moon.*

Step Six: Shuffle the Deck

Using a tarot or oracle deck, pull a simple three card spread.

- The first card will represent where you are today.
- The second card represents what may be blocking or limiting you.
- The third card represents a possible solution or tool to accomplish your New Moon wishes.

Write about your understanding of the cards you pulled, then set some additional intentions based on what you discover. Trust the magic!

Step Seven: Closing Sacred Space

It is important to seal the energy after any ceremony. Refer to **page xx** for our suggestion on closing sacred space, or say your personalized closing prayers.

Ancient Powers of Cacao*

Cacao is a tree that bears cacao seeds which can be roasted and ground to form cocoa and other products. Cacao was considered in many ancient cultures in Central and South America as the food of the gods. In Mayan lore, cacao was discovered inside a mythical mountain, a gift to the Mayan people by the Sun God (Hunahpú)). Cacao became one of the most sacred foods of the Maya. Cacao has been used in ceremony to drink, eat or paint on sacrifices. The beans were used as a form of currency because of their value. It was also a drink of the elite, and was used in burial ceremonies for the journey of the dead into the underworld. Cacao has many medicinal purposes—specifically for the bowel or digestive system and kidneys. Cacao in ceremony is used to unlock enlightened visions and astral or out-of-body travel.

*Note the gift of cacao from the "Sun" god and its relation to the Solar Plexus Chakra that governs the digestive system.

Ritual Cacao Drink Recipe

Add this to any ceremony, or before a meditation for some extra magick.

1. Mix cacao paste/powder with Water.
2. Add optional spices (cinnamon, mint, or chilli pepper).
3. Shake the mixture or blend it until it creates a foam on the top layer.
4. Add optional sweeteners (honey or agave).

Drink at room temperature, or slightly warmed.

MAKING IT PERSONAL

Moon Musings

- Amanda

Gemini falls in my 12th house, so this New Moon is always like eclipse energy for me. It is simultaneously a time of both beginnings and endings. It's a Moon where I strive to face fears, especially the ones created in my magic, magnifying mind or subconscious thought-processes that limit my peace, joy, and connection with my Higher Power. Here are a few musings I have used in previous Gemini New Moons:

- My head and my heart are aligned with clarity, love, peace, and divine intelligence in all interactions. I am peace of mind. I am peace of heart.
- I shift into higher levels of consciousness, awareness, and vitality through patience and focused intentions aligned with my beliefs. I am a conscious and conscientious co-creator of a loving reality.
- I offer my divine love and intelligence unconditionally to my clients, audience and the multiverse, letting go of attachments to outcomes and expectations. I am in radical acceptance of all that ever was and will be.
- Anything buried beneath the surface of my conscious awareness is rooted out, brought to light, and processed in the highest, healthiest light, in line with my higher self and for the greatest good.
- The thoughts I think count. I am aware of my mind-body connection. I give thanks to my biological intelligence.

Best Wishes

- Tiffany

The New Moon in Gemini hits in my 6th or 7th house depending on the degree of the New Moon. So, sometimes I add elements relating to health (6th house) or relationships (7th house). Here are a few wishes I have used on previous Gemini New Moons:

- Spellbound Publishers attracts amazing authors who bring enlightenment to Earth and who are easy and fun to work with.
- I maintain right relationships with everyone in my life through healthy, effective communication that is kind, powerful, and heart-centered.
- I accept clear logic in my relationship with (XYZ) through positive, loving interactions.

- I easily learn yogic principles, philosophies, postures, and pranayama as I relax into a new way of life through yoga teacher training.
- I am clear, confident, and kind when communicating with others.
- I easily connect with a fun and professional writers group to help me reach my writing goals. *[I belong to a self-named group called the Gemini Moon Writers Group.]*
- I have time to map out and schedule thoughtful newsletters that make a positive impact on the readers.
- Above all, help me set aside what I think I know, and what I think I want, so that the Divine can flow through me. May I be of service to God and my fellows.

Word to the Wise: The yoga wish was made in May of 2019 and came true in July 2019! Upon signing up for the training, I created a new intention: "My intention for participating in yoga teacher training is for this to be a personal quest to recalibrate my life force energy and vitality, elevating what I'm capable of mentally, physically, emotionally, spiritually, and relationally, deeply bonding and connecting to my highest self, shifting my consciousness towards enlightenment, centering myself in sacred, ancient, and profound wisdom, and resetting my integrity around divine right relationship, connection with the natural kingdom, others, and myself —rooted in truth and love." After this intention I chose to eat a mostly vegan diet, began a daily meditation routine, and started teaching yoga classes.

Cancer New Moon

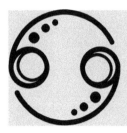

WHEN THE NEW MOON IS IN CANCER

When the New Moon falls in the Water sign of Cancer, you can expect emotional intelligence to reign supreme. Cancer is the Moon's home sign, and Luna is quite comfortable here. You may feel like nesting and finding comfort in home-cooked meals, keeping the home Fires burning. If you notice controlling behaviors and obsessive-compulsive patterns, that's part of the bad behaviors of this Moon sign— consider where you can let someone off the hook. This is the perfect Moon to initiate a new project for your home, conduct a house blessing, or change your address numerology. This is the Moon of the Mother archetype as well as the Intuitive Counselor. There is a yearning to nurture and be nurtured. It's time to bang the drum of self-care and healthy relationships. *Visit www.WiseSkiesAdvice.com for our House or Business Blessing.*

Cancer is the fourth sign of the zodiac and is represented by the Crab. It is a Water sign, ruled by the Moon.

Positive (High) Vibes of the Cancer New Moon

(*Make wishes in these areas*)

Home and family
Cooking, nurturing and mothering
Caring and caregiving
Kindness and compassion
Emotional intelligence
Keen intuition and gut instincts
Empathy and sensitivity to others
Healing early childhood conditioning
Creating space for self-compassion

Challenging (Low) Vibes of the Cancer New Moon

(*What you might wish to remove*)

Being controlling

Perfectionism
Being over-protective
Insecurity
Obsessiveness
Fear of rejection
Lack of clear ambitions
Being moody or crabby

In Health, Cancer Governs

Chest
Breast
Ribs
Stomach
Pancreas
Tumors
Digestive system
Third Eye (Anja)
Heart Chakra (Anahata)

Sample Wishes for the New Moon in Cancer

- I easily allow myself to feel nurtured by others.
- I'm comfortable in my home, and in my own skin.
- I embrace a total healing in the area of chest and lungs.

Cancer New Moon Intention

I openly discover parts of myself that are genuine, kind, and compassionate and find opportunities to unconditionally share them with others. I am courageously open, honest, and true.

Cancer New Moon Healing Invocation

I invoke sacred healing space for the processes of my body and the optimal biological and physiological function of my digestive system. I breathe expansively into my chest, expanding my ribcage and filling my lungs with rich, healthy oxygen. Healing flows to and through me.

Word to the Wise

When the Moon is in Cancer, it's possible you are feeling heightened emotions, increased intuition, and more empathy. Depending on your personal constituency and situation, you may enjoy the emotional depth provided under a Water-Moon. But if things are feeling too heavy, you can incorporate elements from the opposite sign throughout the day to balance things out. The opposite sign of Cancer is Capricorn. Consider drumming, walking on the ground outside with bare feet, or visualizing roots growing through your feet to the center of the Earth in meditation to combine emotions (Water) with stability and practical outcomes (Earth). Combining Water and Earth elements assists you in anchoring your intentions with practical action.

Working with Corresponding Elements

We suggest using one or more items of your choice from each element when designing your ceremony. Use as many or as few as you like.

CANCER **Fire** items: Candles + Smoke

- Candles (white or off-white) - calming
- Natural scented candles, herbal bundles, or incense:
  - Cedar incense - connection
  - Sage - clearing

CANCER **Earth** items: Crystals + Stones

- Rose Quartz - unconditional love
- Rhodonite - compassion
- Moonstone - intuition
- Pink or Watermelon Tourmaline - emotional clarity

CANCER **Air** items: Intentions + Mantras

- Any personal wishes you want to make in the areas Cancer governs + the High Vibe Aspects of Cancer
- Cancer New Moon Intention
- Cancer New Moon Healing Invocation

CANCER **Water** items: Essential Oils + Flower Essences

- Rosemary - passion
- Fennel - cleansing

- Cinnamon - heart health
- Juniper - healing

CANCER NEW MOON NUMEROLOGY

There are many ways to incorporate numerology when formulating your ceremony. You can find numbers to work with in the degree of the sign, the date, the hour you conduct the ceremony, etc. The New Moon Numerology Empowerment Code is a special formula developed by Amanda Rieger Green at Wise Skies. We like to think of this as part of our secret sauce. We use this number to find synchronicities as well as journaling on the day of the New Moon.

Cancer New Moon Numerology Empowerment Code = 8

Numbers have power. We add the numbers that correlate with the Sun sign and the Moon sign, to create a unique code to use in ceremonies. During the New Moon, the Sun and the Moon appear in the same zodiac sign. That means each one is assigned the same number as the zodiac sign of Cancer.

The Wise Skies Formula:
Cancer Numerology Code = 4
Sun in Cancer (4) + Moon in Cancer (4) = 8

The "8" Empowerment Code promotes abundance, self-worth, and manifestation.

Notice when you see an 8 today: it's a reminder to stay open-minded to opportunities of abundance. Seeing an 8 reminds you to pause and thank your lucky stars. It can enhance your ceremony to incorporate 8 of anything in your design.

Numerology Code Journaling

- *What does abundance feel like to me? When do I feel abundant?*
- *Am I willing to recognize and honor myself with honesty, love, and compassion in the energies of this Cancer New Moon in order to clearly manifest more abundance in my inner and outer life?*

The New Moon in Cancer is an ideal time to change the vibe of your home. You can do this without packing up and moving by using the magic of address numerology. Changing the vibration of your home is supremely simple and an amazingly effective way to create a beautiful change in your living space. Seriously, it just takes a few steps, and does not require contacting the post office to change your address. All it takes is a post-it note! Learn more through the ceremony below. Dive deep by getting a copy of *Numerology for Your Home*, by Amanda Rieger Green at www.WiseSkiesAdvice.com.

CANCER NEW MOON CEREMONY
Home Sweet Home

This ceremony teaches you how to use address numerology to shift the vibe of your home or work environment. This is a powerful way to align the energies of your space with your goals and dreams, using number codes to support the manifestation of intentions. The Cancer New Moon is ideal timing for this ceremony, but you can do it on any New Moon, at the beginning of the new year, on the first of the month, and for moving into a new home.

BEFORE YOU BEGIN GATHERING TOOLS, SAY THE NEW MOON INVOCATION FOUND ON PAGE XX.

Step One: Selecting Tools

Set up a New Moon wishing area in a quiet space without distractions. Ideally you can do this outdoors, but a private space inside works too. Refer to the corresponding elements in the section above to select your tools. We suggest incorporating at least one tool per element (Fire, Earth, Air, Water), as well as a journal to write your intentions and responses to the journal prompts. You'll also need a post-it note and a sage wand if you're changing your address numerology and blessing your home.

Step Two: Determine Your Address Numerology

Address Numerology is the art of using the numbers in your address to understand and shift the feeling you get when you're in that particular space.

First, determine the current energy in your home by calculating your address numerology.

Add up the numbers of your address, then reduce it all to a single digit. Example: 2705 Canyon Drive

Add or sum up the numbers:
2 + 7 + 0 + 5 = 14
Reduce it: 1 + 4 = 5
For this address, the vibration is a 5.

Step Three: Feeling at Home

Next, you will need to determine what energy you're wanting to feel in your home life. This is no small thing—it requires discernment of your goals and desires.

Here is a quick review of the vibes behind each number:

1 = Individuality
2 = Partnership
3 = Creativity
4 = Process and analysis
5 = Adventure
6 = Nurturing
7 = Wisdom seeking
8 = Value and abundance
9 = Integrity

Refer to **pages XYX** to better understand the attributes of each number.

Step Four: Easy Math

Once you've determined what number you want "more" of in your home, take the vibe number of your current address and figure out what number you would need to add to it so that the sum would reduce down or sum up to the number you want. Let's continue with the following example.

Say for instance your current address vibration is a 5 (adventure) and you want your address to have the vibe of a 2 (partnership).

So, what do you add to 5 to equal 2?
No, this isn't a trick question.

The answer is 6 (It's a base 9 system! For non-math people, a clock is a base 12 system that you use every day.) 5 + 6 = 11 Reduce the eleven to get your two: 1 + 1 = 2

Let's do one more example with your address as a 5. Perhaps you want your address to be a 9 (integrity). What do you add to 5 to equal 9? The answer is 4. Why? 5 + 4 = 9

Step Five: Meditate

Light a candle. Dab a few drops of essential oil(s) on your left index finger. Rub this on the back of your neck, your throat, and the base of your spine. This will activate the root (home, safety, security) and throat (clear communication) chakras.

Breathe in for three seconds.
Hold your breath for three seconds.
Breathe out for three seconds.
Hold your breath for three seconds.
Repeat this three times.

Say: *It is my intention that this home will embody the essence and highest vibrations of the number _____. (Now state some of the words/energies associated with the number that you want to call into your home.)*

Step Six: Set Intentions

Pull inspiration and insights from the properties of Cancer (as listed above in the sample wishes, the areas Cancer governs + the High Vibe Aspects of Cancer) to write up to ten intentions in your journal. This is also an ideal time to write the New Moon Intention and the Healing Invocation. Reminder: the most potent time for wish-making is within eight hours of the New Moon. Invitation: Write one strong intention for your home.

Step Seven: Post-it Note

As calculated above (for example), you wanted to add a "6" to your 5 (adventure)-address to bring more vibes of 2 (partnership) into your home. All you need to do is get a post-it note and write the number "6" on it.

Note: Do <u>not</u> simply write the number that you're wanting more of (in this instance, the number 2 for partnership). You will unintentionally affect the numerology in a completely different way than you are intending to change. Instead, be sure you write the number that actually changes the energy of your home to the energy of partnership, which in this instance is the number "6".

Write your intention for your home, or your favorite New Moon wish, on the back side of the post-it note. Write the number needed to add to your current number on the front side, then stick it to the inside of the doorframe of your front door within the first eight hours of the New Moon in Cancer. This is the most potent portal of the year to change the way your home feels.

Yes, that's all you have to do! Trust us, it works. The energy field of your home is now changing. Give it a week or two (sometimes it can be sooner) and you will begin to notice a difference in the energy of your home. Put your intentions to work and trust the process. Prepare to be amazed.

Note: If you're interested in learning more about the basics of numerology and address numerology, check out our sister book in this series: *Numerology For Your Home*, by Amanda Rieger Green, MPH.

*Option: Sage your house. After you place the post-it on the door, you can sage the house and say a blessing. Need ideas? See our home blessing ceremony at www.WiseSkiesAdvice.com for invocations to bless the new energy of your home.

Step Eight: Closing Sacred Space

It is important to seal the energy after any ceremony. Refer to **page xx** for our suggestion on closing sacred space, or say your personalized closing prayers.

MAKING IT PERSONAL

Moon Musings

- Amanda

Cancer is my rising sign and I love feeling all the feelings that accompany this energy. It's always a Moon where I work with my emotional and biological intelligence to create more authenticity, fulfillment, and nurture. I usually incorporate an epsom salt scrub cleansing the morning after this New Moon to ground into my emotional body and rearticulate my personal boundaries and New Moon intentions. Cancer Moons are highly empathic, so this is a complementary action. Here are a few musings from previous Cancer New Moons:

- I am in tune with my cosmic and grounded intuition, paying attention to all the signs and synchronicities. I trust the magic of the multiverse.
- I organically crave high vibrational foods that nourish my mind, body, and soul.
- I experience compassion, snuggles and sweet moments of presence with my dogs, thanking them for the special space they hold for me

each and everyday. Their unconditional energies are contagious in my energy field and attitude.

- I AM love.
- Nurture, compassion and patience flows through my being naturally. My heart chakra is open and receptive.

Word to the Wise: Epsom salt is a great tool to keep close to the tub or shower. Grab a handful after you're fully bathed. Scrub your body with it, head to toe. Say aloud (it's important to say this aloud so your DNA and cells hear the frequency of your voice): "I am cleansing and clearing my energy. Any lower vibrational frequencies are now shifting into more love, intelligence, and consciousness." You can do this a couple of times a week or when you intuitively feel inclined.

Best Wishes

- Tiffany

The New Moon in Cancer hits in my 7th or 8th house depending on the degree of the New Moon. So sometimes I add elements relating to relationships (7th house) or shared resources (8th house). Here are a few wishes I have used on previous Cancer New Moons:

- I feel comfortable, radiant, and at home in my body.
- Yoga and meditation enhance my vitality and sense of connection between mind-body-spirit.
- My intuition and mediumship gifts are clear, strong, and easy to access.
- I thrive on simple and interesting vegan foods that delight me, nourish me, and taste good.
- I have a welcoming nature that helps people feel at home within themselves.
- I love the evolution of my home and garden space that feels mystical and enhances my ability to grow spiritually while in communion with nature.
- I am deeply connected to the Divine Mother energy, my mom, my children, my grandmothers, as well as my own ancient and sacred mother-energy.
- Above all, help me set aside what I think I know, and what I think I want, so that the Divine can flow through me. May I be of service to God and my fellows.

Word to the Wise: If you're working with address numerology – buckle up! I have followed Amanda's advice for changing the numerology of my home during this potent portal and had dramatic results each time. During house blessings, use a bell, singing bowl, or tuning fork in the corners to shift any stagnant energy. I also recommend pouring salt in bowls in the four corners of your house, and placing special crystals in a grid between the salt bowls. Add any special dried herbs to your salt bowl (I like holy basil and rosemary).

Leo New Moon

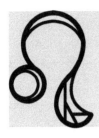

WHEN THE NEW MOON IS IN LEO

When the New Moon falls in the Fire sign of Leo, you can expect passions to surface. You might notice extra energy around entertainment, including some spirited and assertive vibes. This is the perfect Moon to set an intention around playfulness and having more fun with life. This is the Moon of the heart-centered leader. It's time to bang the drum of courage and look at the world through rose colored glasses. Everyone deserves more unconditional Leo-like love, not less.

Leo is the fifth sign in the zodiac and is represented by the Lion. It is a Fire sign, ruled by the Sun.

Positive (High) Vibes of the Leo New Moon

(*Make wishes in these areas*)

Leadership
Courage
Passionate Play
Loyalty
Generosity
Appreciation
Falling in love with life
Igniting and activating vitality in your DNA
Trusting your insights
Willingness

Challenging (Low) Vibes of the Leo New Moon

(*What you might wish to remove*)

Neediness
Attention-seeking tendencies
Self-centered behaviors
Inability to experience and truly express gratitude

Unrealistic expectations

In Health, Leo Governs

(Areas of the body where you might wish for healing)

Heart
Spinal Cord
Crown Chakra (Sahasrara Chakra)
Heart Chakra (Anahata Chakra)

Sample Wishes for the New Moon in Leo

- I enjoy putting my best foot forward, and standing in my personal power.
- I accept the responsibility of leadership with confidence and courage.
- I find myself having fun with life on a daily basis.

Leo New Moon Intention

I am consciously and lovingly aware of my thoughts, feelings, and physical body, while allowing heart-centered growth and healing. I am empowered through gratitude and humility.

Leo New Moon Healing Invocation

I invoke sacred healing space to and through my heart. My heart heals with laughter, joyful interactions, playful people and generosity. These feelings and experiences organically manifest when my heart is closed off. Healing happens through the love I unconditionally give and receive.

Word to the Wise

When the Moon is in Leo, you are likely feeling hot, and possibly looking for attention and affection. Depending on your personal constituency and situation, you may enjoy the Fire energy. But if things are feeling too heated, you can incorporate elements from the opposite sign throughout the day to balance things out. The opposite sign of Leo is the Air sign Aquarius. Consider contemplative activities like a walking meditation in a labyrinth to combine action (Fire) with mindfulness (Air). Getting into action (Leo) for groups (Aquarius) through volunteerism is another idea to encourage equilibrium.

Working with Corresponding Elements

We suggest using one or more items of your choice from each element when designing your ceremony. Use as many or as few as you like.

LEO **Fire** items: Candles + Smoke

- Yellow or white candles - empowerment
- Citrus scented candles, herbal bundles, incense
    - Orange, Lemon, Grapefruit - uplifting
    - Sage - cleansing
    - Palo Santo - protection

LEO **Earth** items: Crystals + Stones

- Citrine - abundance
- Carnelian - emotional intelligence
- Moss Agate - soothing
- Pyrite - processing
- Fuchsite - head and heart
- Sunstone - vitality

LEO **Air** items: Intentions + Mantras

- Any personal wishes you want to make in the areas Leo governs + the High Vibe Aspects of Leo
- Leo New Moon Intention
- Leo New Moon Healing Invocation

LEO **Water** items: Essential Oils + Flower Essences

- Cinnamon Oil - healing
- Tea Tree Oil - raising your vibration
- Frankincense - royalty
- Lemon - manifestation

LEO NEW MOON NUMEROLOGY

There are many ways to incorporate numerology when formulating your ceremony. You can find numbers to work with in the degree of the sign, the date, the hour you conduct the ceremony, etc. The New Moon Numerology Empowerment Code is a special formula developed by Amanda Rieger Green, MPH at Wise Skies. We like to think of this as part of our secret sauce. We

use this number to find synchronicities as well as journaling on the day of the New Moon.

Leo New Moon Numerology Empowerment Code = 1

Numbers have power. We add the numbers that correlate with the Sun sign and the Moon sign, to create a unique code to use in ceremonies. During the New Moon, the Sun and the Moon appear in the same zodiac sign. That means each one is assigned the same number as the zodiac sign of Leo.

The Wise Skies Formula:
Leo Numerology Code = 5
Sun in Leo (5) + Moon in Leo (5) = 10
Reduce it to a single digit: 1+0 = 1

The "1" Empowerment Code promotes individuality, a pioneering spirit and futuristic vision. Notice when you see a 1 today: it's a reminder to put yourself first. Seeing a 1 reminds you to pause and put your oxygen mask on before helping others. It can enhance your ceremony to incorporate 1 of anything in your design.

Numerology Code Journaling

- *Who am I?*
- *When do I authentically express my individuality?*
- *How can I courageously integrate my vision into this Leo New Moon energy?*

LEO NEW MOON CEREMONY

Igniting the Cosmic Heart

*This ceremony summons courage and bravery through heartfelt intentions using crystal magic. This ceremony is ideal for empowering you to put your best foot forward, love unconditionally, and stand in your personal power. See Amanda's Leo New Moon story on **page xxx!***

BEFORE YOU BEGIN GATHERING TOOLS, SAY THE NEW MOON INVOCATION FOUND ON PAGE XX.

Step One: Selecting Tools

Set up a New Moon wishing area in a quiet space without distractions. Ideally you can do this outdoors, but a private space inside works too. Refer to the corresponding elements in the section above to select your tools. We suggest incorporating at least one tool per element (Fire, Earth, Air, Water), as well as a journal to write your intentions and responses to the journal prompts.

Step Two: Fire & Smoke

Light the sage, palo santo, or candle, and allow the smoke to clear your energy. Carefully cover and cleanse your entire body and energy field with the smoke or scent of the candle. You can clear the energy of the recommended crystals, oils, and your journal by waving them in the smoke or above the flame of the candle.

Say: *I am cleansing and clearing my energy, allowing all lower vibrations to shift into the highest light. I am clear.*

Once finished, close your eyes. Inhale and exhale deeply three times to reset your energy field.

Step Three: Oil Bath

Choose the oil(s) with the energy or traits you wish to blend with your energy field. Dab a few drops of essential oil(s) on your palms. Rub your palms together creating heat, then raise your palms in front of your face, inhaling deeply.

Inhale deeply, then say: *I am courageous.*

Exhale deeply, then say: *I am truthful.*

Again, rub your palms together to generate energy and scent from the oil(s). Next, gently swirl your hands around the top of your head and down your body to the bottom of your feet—bathing in the scent and energy of the oil from head to toe. Repeat until you feel your energy body infused with the scent and energy of the oil.

Note: Be mindful of the oils and do not get them near your eyes or on places that can irritate your skin.

Step Four: Activation

Find a comfortable seat (on a chAir or the floor), outside if possible. Place the crystals you are working with in your palms. Close your eyes and imagine there is a beautiful ray of golden liquid light streaming down from the Sun coming directly in through the crown of the head (Crown Chakra) and immersing your entire body with love, light, and intelligence. Imagine that the wisdom of the cosmos is activating your DNA and infusing light into your cells.

Silently ask the crystals to interact with the Sun's light rays and communicate any necessary information and intelligence you need to hear on this Leo New Moon. Take your time. Breathe in and out deeply. Notice any sensations in the crown of your head or the palms of your hands.

Note: we all receive messages differently. You may see colors, hear words, feel sensations, or notice the presence of your spirit guides. You may also sense nothing, and that is ok. Trust whatever you experience as part of the process..

Step Five: Higher Self

Now, connect with your higher self and silently ask: "Please set aside my ego's desires, so that I can hear what is most important for my soul's evolution in this moment." Next, ask your divine support team to offer any additional information or insights to guide you in understanding what you need to know and do for your soul's evolution this month. Once you feel you have received your guidance, offer thanks.

Step Six: Set Intentions

Pull inspiration and insights from your meditation, the New Moon numerology, our sample wishes, and the properties of Leo to write up to ten intentions in your journal. Reminder: the Leo energy supports you in activating courage, leadership, shining your unique light in the world, as well as generosity with your time and talents. Take a small piece of paper and write down key words from one main wish: the thing that you most feel called to work with at this time.

Step Seven: Sealing The Energy of Your Intentions

Relight your sage, palo santo, or candle. Wave your piece of paper through the smoke, stating: "It is my intention that this wish is pure and of the highest light. I trust my higher self to embody the words on this page in divine right timing. And so it is."

Step Eight: Crystal Magic

Set the crystals on top of your journal in the darkness of the New Moon for the number of nights associated with Leo Numerology (1). This allows them to recharge their energy and to support your intentions. If you cannot leave the crystals and journal outside, you can put them in a window sill.

In the morning, retrieve the crystals with gratitude. Keep the crystals in your pocket, next to your bed, in your car, or somewhere close over the next few weeks. Continue communication with the crystals, acknowledging them and thanking them for their support and intelligence.

Option: Discipline and routine are key to effectively and fully engaging with the universal energies. Commit to opening your journal every morning for the next (1) week. With crystals in hand, read your New Moon intentions out loud. You can also keep the recommended essential oils close by and breathe in their scent and energy. This not only engages your muscle memory, it sends a signal to the universe that you are intentionally aligning your energies with your intentions with great commitment. You can even relight your candle or incense during this time. Make it your own morning ceremony and see what unfolds.

Step Nine: Closing Sacred Space

It is important to seal the energy after any ceremony. Refer to **page xx** for our suggestion on closing sacred space, or say your personalized closing prayers.

MAKING IT PERSONAL

Moon Musings

- Amanda

I have a whole lot of Leo lessons in my life. My North Node is in Leo, my mother and one of my sisters are strong representations of Leo bravery, courage, generosity and show for me. Embracing those energies for myself isn't always so easy. This New Moon energy is always a cornerstone of the year in embracing my karmic direction. Here are a few musings I have used on previous Leo New Moons:

- I will author a book in the course of the next year, and courageously create more tools and teaching opportunities for raising the vibration of the planet through divine partnerships and love.
- I am bold and courageous in my actions and impressions. I allow myself to be seen.
- I shine from the inside out.
- The time I spend with my mother is of quality, love, joy and healing. I am present without strings throughout her healing process. No regrets.
- I laugh often. My laughter reverberates throughout the Multiverse and my simultaneous lives.
- Need more real world ideas? You can also find my *Leo New Moon story on **page xxx!***

Note: I hosted 75 people on my property in Austin, TX for the August 2017 Great American Eclipse, which was in 21° Leo (21 = creativity through interconnection and communication). We moved through an empowering, cleansing and activating yoga practice, we spoke intentions rhythmically, one after another, and activated a massive crystal grid. It was truly a Leo New Moon to remember. Then I set this intention. Within the next 6 months (eclipse energy triggers a 6 month cycle), Tiffany and I collaborated to form Wise Skies Advice, and my first book was published in 2018.

Best Wishes

- Tiffany

The New Moon in Leo hits in my 8th or 9th house depending on the degree of the New Moon. So sometimes I add elements relating to shared resources (8th house) or philosophy and publishing (9th house). Here are a few wishes I have used on previous Leo New Moons:

- It is my intention to be clear, honest, loving, supportive, present, strong, and in loving service to my parents.
- I enjoy engaging my North Node in Leo, and having fun with life.
- I take heart-centered action through leadership.
- Above all, help me set aside what I think I know, and what I think I want, so that the Divine can flow through me. May I be of service to God and my fellows.

Virgo New Moon

WHEN THE NEW MOON IS IN VIRGO

When the New Moon falls in the Earth sign of Virgo, you can expect some extra wit, wisdom, and volunteerism. You might find yourself putting energy into organization, your health, and the details of life. This is the perfect Moon to find practical solutions, get grounded, and start a new health regimen. This is the Moon of the practical thinker, the helper, and the herbalist. It's time to bang the drum of being reasonable and look at the world with the fine print in mind.

Virgo is the sixth sign of the zodiac and is represented by the Virgin. It is an Earth sign, ruled by Mercury and Chiron.

Positive (High) Vibes of the Virgo New Moon

(*Make wishes in these areas*)

Integrity
Practicality
Precision
Being of service
Organization
Constructive criticism
Trusting the process
Blending the old with the new
Setting up new procedures

Challenging (Low) Vibes of the Virgo New Moon

(*What you might wish to remove*)

Judgmental or overly critical attitudes
Analysis paralysis
Inefficiency or getting stuck in the details
Inability to see the bigger picture

In Health, Virgo Governs

(Areas of the body where you might wish for healing)
Kidneys
Intestines
Abdomen
Solar Plexus (Manipura Chakra)
Throat Chakra (Vishudha Chakra)

Sample Wishes for the New Moon in Virgo

- I enjoy creating order and functionality in my new filing system at work.
- I easily get an appointment with the right health care practitioner who can most effectively help me return to a state of full vitality.
- I love finding positive, playful angles when digging into the minutiae of life.

Virgo New Moon Intention

I joyfully use my innate gifts, sharing them with others freely, trusting others through the process, learning lessons along the way, and finding peace. I am simultaneously self-confident and humble in my thoughts and actions. I am ready for a house cleaning of the heart.

Virgo New Moon Healing Invocation

I invoke sacred healing space from the inside of my being and my body, organically purifying my kidneys and intestines, optimizing my abdominal cavity to support and heal my mind, body, and spirit. My healing is a journey that begins from within.

Word to the Wise

When the Moon is in Virgo, you are likely feeling practical and grounded. Depending on your personal constituency and situation, you may enjoy the security and stability the Earth energy provides. But if things are feeling dense, fixed, or even stuck, you can incorporate elements from the opposite sign throughout the day to balance things out. The opposite sign of Virgo is the Water sign Pisces. Consider Water-related activities to encourage fluidity and motion: taking baths, drinking tea, making spritzes, using herbal sprays and tinctures, swimming in hot springs or a lake. It can be useful to combine the steadfastness of your intentions (Earth) with the flexibility of trusting providence to flow in at divine right timing (Water).

Working with Corresponding Elements

We suggest using one or more items of your choice from each element when designing your ceremony. Use as many or as few as you like.

VIRGO **Fire** items: Candles + Smoke

- Grey and green candles - giving
- Herbal and Earthy scented candles, herbal bundes, or incense:
    - Rosemary - passion
    - Sage - clearing
    - Thyme - grounding
    - Olive - purity

VIRGO **Earth** items: Crystals + Stones

- Amethyst - anti-anxiety
- Chrysocolla - Earth connection
- Moss Agate - peace
- Citrine - focus
- Celestite - healing

VIRGO **Air** items: Intentions + Mantras

- Any personal wishes you want to make in the areas Virgo governs + the High Vibe Aspects of Virgo
- Virgo New Moon Intention
- Virgo New Moon Healing Invocation

VIRGO **Water** items: Essential Oils + Flower Essences

- Peppermint - excitement
- Grapefruit - kindness
- Sandalwood - spirituality
- Chamomile - peace

VIRGO NEW MOON NUMEROLOGY

There are many ways to incorporate numerology when formulating your ceremony. You can find numbers to work with in the degree of the sign, the date, the hour you conduct the ceremony, etc. The New Moon Numerology

Empowerment Code is a special formula developed by Amanda Rieger Green, MPH at Wise Skies. We like to think of this as part of our secret sauce. We use this number to find synchronicities as well as journaling on the day of the New Moon.

Virgo New Moon Numerology Empowerment Code = 3

Numbers have power. We add the numbers that correlate with the Sun sign and the Moon sign, to create a unique code to use in ceremonies. During the New Moon, the Sun and the Moon appear in the same zodiac sign. That means each one is assigned the same number as the zodiac sign of Virgo.

The Wise Skies Formula:
Virgo Numerology Code = 6
Sun in Virgo (6) + Moon in Virgo (6) = 12
Reduce it to a single digit: 1+2 = 3

The "3" Empowerment Code promotes creativity, communication, and socialization. Notice when you see a 3 today: it's a reminder to get creative. Seeing a 3 reminds you to pause and think outside the box. It can enhance your ceremony to incorporate 3 of anything in your design.

Numerology Code Journaling

- *When do I feel my most creative?*
- *Am I comfortable communicating my creativity?*
- *How can I best express myself in healthy, supportive social circles during this Virgo New Moon?*

VIRGO NEW MOON CEREMONY
Practical Magic

This ceremony uses the healing powers of herbs and crystals to purify and magnify your intentions around organization, practicality, and efficiency. It can be replicated in your garden, on your property, at a business location, or it can even be used to bless a specific room throughout the year.

BEFORE YOU BEGIN GATHERING TOOLS, SAY THE NEW MOON INVOCATION FOUND ON PAGE XX.

Step One: Selecting Tools

Set up a New Moon wishing area in a quiet space without distractions. Ideally you can do this outdoors, but a private space inside works too. Refer to the corresponding elements in the section above to select your tools. We suggest incorporating at least one tool per element (Fire, Earth, Air, Water), as well as a journal to write your intentions and responses to the journal prompts. You may also want various herbs like sage or rosemary to make your own herbal bundle.

Step Two: Herbal Bundle

Gather fresh herbs from your home garden or the grocery store. You can use an array of herbs such as sage, oregano, and thyme with your rosemary. Add in any other herbs you feel drawn to under this Virgo New Moon energy. Bundle the herbs into a sweet bouquet by wrapping a long string around the bundle, and tying the bundle together off at the base of the herbs (by the stems).

Option: You can certainly purchase an herbal bundle or sage bundle to save time, but there is something special we like about putting our own magick into the bundle.

Step Three: Aromatic Inspiration + Blessing

Light a green or grey candle. Gather the Virgo New Moon crystals, placing them next to you. Finding a comfortable seat, bring the herbal bundle up to your nose and deeply inhale and exhale for three cycles to center yourself.

Say: *Inspire my senses and present me with a new found presence of being. Show me a new and invigorated perspective.*

Meditate quietly for 5-10 minutes.

Step Four: Write Intentions

Using the intention, sample wishes, and prompts from the section above, contemplate the wishes you would like to make. Spend a little quiet time with your herbs and crystals. When you're ready, write out your intentions. Remember, the most optimal time to make wishes is within the first 8 hours of the New Moon being exact.

Step Five: Herb + Crystal Grid

Dab the essential oil(s) on your palms. Rub them together briskly nine times, generating heat and releasing the essential oils into your energy field. Bring your right hand to the crown of your head and your left hand to your belly. Breathe in and out three times.

Say: *I am connected with the Earth. I offer and receive the energies of Earth's living library. I am rooted and connected throughout all space and time.*

Place your herb bundle on top of your intentions or journal outside (or inside near a window). Intuitively place your crystals around the herb bundle and intentions. Once you have your herb and crystal grid, you will need to activate its energies. Touching each crystal with your right index finger, move in a clockwise direction.

Say: *I activate my intentions in the energies of the Virgo New Moon.*

Once you have made it to each crystal and you are back to the crystal you started with,

Say: *And so it is.*

Leave the herb and crystal grid intact, allowing it to charge for 3 days and nights.

Step Six: Drying Out

After 3 days and nights (Virgo Empowerment Code = 3), go to your herb and crystal grid. Spend a few minutes meditating and reconnecting with the energy of the grid and your intentions. Write out any observations about your intentions and insights, dreams, or synchronicities that may have bubbled up over the past 3 days.

Offer gratitude, then take the herb bundle and hang it somewhere sacred to dry out until the Virgo Full Moon (approximately 6 months) or until you're ready to use them. You can place the crystals beside your bed or under your pillow for the next 3 weeks to sync up with their energy and support your intentions.

Step Seven: Closing Sacred Space

Refer to page xx

MAKING IT PERSONAL

Moon Musings

- Amanda

My natal Jupiter and Venus are in Virgo. Virgo season is always the climactic energy leading up to my Libra Solar return. It's usually an intense season of the culmination of lessons in love, compassion, healing and awareness. No big thing, right? This is the New Moon where I personally push through the superficial and dig into the karmic lessons I've encountered over the year. Here are a few musings I have used on previous Virgo New Moons:

- It is my intention that I observe with an eye of objectivity, seeing things from all angles in order to tap into discernment of mind, body and spirit.
- The clients who collaborate with me are seeking greater levels of awareness, personal and spiritual evolution, and cultivating a sense of meaning and truth. I trust the divine orchestration of the Universe.
- I love and honor the body I created for myself in this lifetime, willingly filling it with optimal sources of nourishment, healthy physical activity and kind affirmations of its biological and spiritual intelligence. When my body is pure, my heart and mind are pure.
- I diligently, efficiently and consistently write and share content that offers higher vibrational tools and resources through Wise Skies, Spellbound and Soul Pathology.

- I clean and clear any clutter from my physical environment, mental cognition, emotional space and universal consciousness that limit the purity of joyful creation.

Best Wishes

- Tiffany

The New Moon in Virgo hits in my 9th or 10th house depending on the degree of the New Moon. So sometimes I add elements relating to my big adventure, publishing, or worldview (9th house) or career and public standing (10th house) issues. Here are a few wishes I have used on previous Virgo New Moons:

- I am excited about new yoga flows and the magic pulsing prayers we create when practicing together.
- My Fall garden is enchanting, medicinal, and spellbinding.
- I deeply enjoy connecting with people who want to focus on launching their books this season in an organized, practical approach.
- I renew my commitment to my morning routine.
- I have fun organizing our home with magical housekeeping, numerology, and feng shui.
- I easily attract the best herbalists and vegans to learn from and work with as I expand my knowledge of medicinal tools.
- Above all, help me set aside what I think I know, and what I think I want, so that the Divine can flow through me. May I be of service to God and my fellows.

Libra New Moon

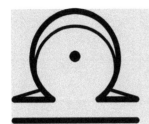

WHEN THE NEW MOON IS IN LIBRA

When the New Moon falls in the Air sign of Libra, you can expect to feel supported. You might notice more beauty, balance, and harmony. This is the perfect Moon to redecorate, set partnership intentions, and explore areas that benefit from multiple perspectives. This is the Moon of the partner and the interior decorator. It's time to bang the drum of friendship and look at the world with fAirness in your eyes.

Libra is the seventh sign in the zodiac and is represented by the Scales. It is an Air sign, ruled by Venus.

Positive (High) Vibes of the Libra New Moon

(*Make wishes in these areas*)

FAirness
Justice
Balance
Harmony
Partnership
Ability to see all perspectives
Kindness
Honesty
Authenticity

Challenging (Low) Vibes of the Libra New Moon

(*What you might wish to remove*)

People-pleasing tendencies
Indecision
Unhealthy compromise
Being two-faced

In Health, Libra Governs

(Areas of the body where you might wish for healing)
Skin
Belly button
Waist
Heart Chakra (Anahata Chakra)

Sample Wishes for the New Moon in Libra

- I easily find balance between my head and my heart.
- I'm treated fAirly in XYZ situation.
- I find myself living the life of my dreams with an amazing partner.
- I embrace a makeover in my house so that my home feels beautiful, inviting, and comfortable.

Libra New Moon Intention

I willingly process life-lessons and practice forgiveness, which creates space for soul-healing, evolution, and an expanded consciousness. I facilitate equality and reciprocity between my head and my heart.

Libra New Moon Healing Invocation

I invoke sacred healing space for balance and harmony in all aspects of my being. My skin, belly button and waist are the core components supporting my health, vitality, and equilibrium. I access the still Waters deep within the core of mySelf for infinite healing.

Word to the Wise

When the Moon is in Libra, it's possible you are seeking fAirness, balance, and beauty. Depending on your personal constituency and situation, you may enjoy the endless options provided under an Air-Moon. But if things are feeling too indecisive and scattered, you can incorporate elements from the opposite sign throughout the day to balance things out. The opposite sign of Libra is Aries (Fire). Consider contemplative yoga or something that combines thought (Air) with action (Fire). Combining Air and Fire elements assists you in transmuting your intentions into the highest and brightest frequencies.

Working with Corresponding Elements

We suggest using one or more items of your choice from each element when designing your ceremony. Use as many or as few as you like.

LIBRA **Fire** items: Candles + Smoke

- Pastel candles (blues, pinks, and purples) - harmony
- Floral and herbal scented candles, herbal bundles, or incense:
  - Sage - clearing
  - Rose - love

LIBRA **Earth** items: Crystals + Stones

- Apatite - decisiveness
- Fluorite - mental clarity
- Green Calcite - beauty
- Chevron Amethyst - wisdom

LIBRA **Air** items: Intentions + Mantras

- Any personal wishes you want to make in the areas Libra governs + the High Vibe Aspects of Libra
- Libra New Moon Intention
- Libra New Moon Healing Invocation

LIBRA **Water** items: Essential Oils + Flower Essences

- Rose - love
- Angelica - dreams
- Geranium - compassion
- Lavender - calm

LIBRA NEW MOON NUMEROLOGY

There are many ways to incorporate numerology when formulating your ceremony. You can find numbers to work with in the degree of the sign, the date, the hour you conduct the ceremony, etc. The New Moon Numerology Empowerment Code is a special formula developed by Amanda Rieger Green, MPH at Wise Skies. We like to think of this as part of our secret sauce. We use this number to find synchronicities as well as journaling on the day of the New Moon.

Libra New Moon Numerology Empowerment Code = 5

Numbers have power. We add the numbers that correlate with the Sun sign and the Moon sign, to create a unique code to use in ceremonies. During the New Moon, the Sun and the Moon appear in the same zodiac sign. That means each one is assigned the same number as the zodiac sign of Libra.

The Wise Skies Formula:
Libra Numerology Code = 7
Sun in Libra (7) + Moon in Libra (7) = 14
Reduce it to a single digit: 1+4 = 5

The "5" Empowerment Code promotes freedom, adventure, and dynamic shifts. Notice when you see a 5 today: it's a reminder to sync up with your inner rebel. Seeing a 5 reminds you to pause and pivot in a new direction. It can enhance your ceremony to incorporate 5 of anything in your design.

Numerology Code Journaling

- *When do I experience freedom?*
- *What does freedom feel like to me?*
- *Am I willing to initiate an adventure and create some dynamic shifts during this Libra New Moon energy in order to experience more freedom?*

LIBRA NEW MOON CEREMONY

Sacred Vision Board

This fun vision board ceremony helps you visualize your intentions into existence. Seeing is believing! In addition to the Libra New Moon, you can use this ceremony on the first day of the new year, on a birthday, or an anniversary.

BEFORE YOU BEGIN GATHERING TOOLS, SAY THE NEW MOON INVOCATION FOUND ON PAGE XX.

Step One: Selecting Tools

Set up a New Moon wishing area in a quiet space without distractions. Ideally you can do this outdoors, but a private space inside works too. Refer to the corresponding elements in the section above to select your tools. We suggest incorporating at least one tool per element (Fire, Earth, Air, Water), as well as a journal to write your intentions and responses to the journal prompts. You'll also want citrus tea, a poster board, glue or tape, magazines, and assorted pens and markers for this ceremony.

Step Two: Set the Stage

Brew a cup of tea for the Libra New Moon. We like rose, citrus, or raspberry, but any tea you like will do the trick. Dab one or more of the New Moon essential oils on your index fingers, and breathe it in. Next, dab the oils on your third eye (center forehead), throat and back of the neck. Hold your choice of crystal(s) in your left palm. The left side is the receptive, feminine side of the body.

Say: *I am inspired. I believe I am worthy of an abundant, fulfilling life—"Believing is Seeing."*

Step Three: Bring Your Vision to Life

Flip through your magazines for inspiration and vision. When you find images, words, phrases, or pictures of people or landscapes that inspire you, cut them out. Remember that vision-boarding is about creating a larger-than-life image and aligning your beliefs with that vision. Dream outside your box. With each image you choose, hold it in your left hand, take one deep inhale and slowly exhale.

Say: *I BELIEVE _____* (fill in the blank with the image or phrase/word).

Tape or glue the clippings in a creative collage on your paper or poster board.

Step Four: Add Intentions and Wishes

Pull inspiration and insights from your meditation, the New Moon numerology, sample wishes, and the properties of Libra to write up to ten intentions on the poster. This is also an ideal spot to write the New Moon Intention and the Healing Invocation. Reminder: The most potent time for wish-making is within eight hours of the New Moon.

Step Five: See it, Write it

Once you have finished your board, spend time journaling on what you want to create, cultivate, and manifest in the energy of the Libra New Moon along with your intentions. We suggest you do this on the back of the vision board. Reminder: Strong Belief + Clear Visualization = Abundant Manifestation.

Step Six: Make it So

Hang your Libra New Moon vision board somewhere of your liking where you will see this imagery often. Hold your Libra New Moon crystals in your right palm. The right side symbolizes the masculine energy of action.

Say: *It is my intention that, each time I see my created vision, I believe that I am capable of manifesting my inspiration into an abundant reality. I trust the process.*

Recommendation: Stay in tune with your innermost dreams and passions by keeping your vision board up for at least 6 months. It's important to revisit your vision (and re-envision) your goals because our desires grow and shift. After 6 months, reflect on what has become a reality, what still lingers, and what new goals you are having. You can recreate this ceremony on another New Moon or on the 1st day of any month.

Step Seven: Closing Sacred Space

It is important to seal the energy after any ceremony. Refer to **page xx** for our suggestion on closing sacred space, or say your personalized closing prayers.

MAKING IT PERSONAL

Moon Musings

- Amanda

The Libra New Moon is not only my birthday Moon, but it's also where my natal Moon was when I jumped off the cosmic diving board. I was born at the moment the Libra new moon was exact. I usually review the prior 12 months from a vitality and selfhood perspective (the Sun) as well as an emotional and subconscious vantage (the Moon). I honor my experience and look forward with my annual intentions. I laugh at how very Libra (balanced, well-rounded perspectives) this whole process is for me! Here are a few intentions and reflections from past Libra New Moons:

- I experience balance and flow in all aspects of my life. I create stability for myself and those around me. I am a stabilizer.
- I honor the expressions of my vitality and selfhood over the past year, accepting both the peaks and valleys as divinely orchestrated for my personal and spiritual evolution.
- I speak my truth. I articulate healthy boundaries. My inside matches my outside.
- Partnerships, friendships, and all relationships evolve into the highest good for all parties.
- Thank you (to the Universe).

Best Wishes

- Tiffany

The New Moon in Libra hits in my 10th or 11th house depending on the degree of the New Moon. So, sometimes I add elements relating to career (10th) or community (11th) related themes. Here are a few wishes I have used on previous Libra New Moons:

- I am tactful and compassionate.
- I respect others' point of view and love them unconditionally.
- I forgive those who owe me.
- I refine my relationships to be fAir, balanced, and fun.
- I crave only foods that are healthy for my body and enhance my life force energy.

- Above all, help me set aside what I think I know, and what I think I want, so that the Divine can flow through me. May I be of service to God and my fellows.

Scorpio New Moon

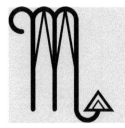

WHEN THE NEW MOON IS IN SCORPIO

When the New Moon falls in the Water sign of Scorpio, things feel intense. You might feel like connecting deeply with one special person, or hiding away for personal time. This is the perfect Moon to initiate a new research project, to set an intention around self-development, or to find an intimate connection. This is the Moon of the alchemist and the power player. It's time to bang the drum of self-transcendence and look at the world with intuitive eyes.

Scorpio is the eighth sign in the zodiac and is represented by the Scorpion. It is a Water sign, ruled by Mars and Pluto.

Positive (High) Vibes of the Scorpio New Moon

(*Make wishes in these areas*)

Ability to execute
Transcendence
Growth
Passion and desire
Resourcefulness
Embracing personality quirks as strengths
Self-discovery
Connection with an intimate partner
Healing power struggles and finding your personal power
Making new financial pathways through shared resources
Magic and metaphysics

Challenging (Low) Vibes of the Scorpio New Moon

(*What you might wish to remove*)

Jealousy
Resentment
Secrecy

Distrust
Revenge

In Health, Scorpio Governs

(Areas of the body where you might wish for healing)

Urinary system
Kidneys
Gallbladder
Sex organs
Elimination organs
Sacral Chakra (Svadhisthana Chakra)

Sample Wishes for the New Moon in Scorpio

- I love finding new classes, workshops, and books that help me learn about my spiritual self.
- It's easy and lucrative to work with others, we are stronger together.
- I enjoy finding magic in the mundane.

Scorpio New Moon Intention

All parts of my karma and spirit interconnect with integrity and serenity. I experience clarity and honesty, trusting divine right timing.

Scorpio New Moon Healing Invocation

I invoke sacred healing space for optimal healing to process organically through my uriniary system, kidneys, gallbladder, sex and elimination organs. My body, mind and spirit are aligned and functioning with peace and ease.

Word to the Wise

When the Moon is in Scorpio, it's possible you are feeling intense emotions and have increased intuition. Your spidey-sense is in full swing. You may notice people are feeling passionate or are more easily triggered. Depending on your personal constituency and situation, you may enjoy the emotional depth provided under a Water-Moon. But if things are feeling too heavy, you can incorporate elements from the opposite sign throughout the day to balance things out. The opposite sign of Scorpio is Taurus. Consider drumming, walking on the ground outside with bare feet, or visualizing roots growing through your feet to the center of the Earth in meditation to combine emotions (Water) with stability and practical outcomes (Earth). Combining Water and Earth elements assists you in anchoring your intentions with practical action.

Working with Corresponding Elements

We suggest using one or more items of your choice from each element when designing your ceremony. Use as many or as few as you like.

SCORPIO **Fire** items: Candles + Smoke

- Black, red, and orange candles - passion
- Heavy scented candles, herbal bundles, or incense:
  - Palo santo - protection
  - Patchouli incense - detoxification

SCORPIO **Earth** items: Crystals + Stones

- Tiger's Eye - empowerment
- Carnelian - emotional intelligence
- Obsidian - energetic clearing
- Peridot - magic

SCORPIO **Air** items: Intentions + Mantras

- Any personal wishes you want to make in the areas Scorpio governs + the High Vibe Aspects of Scorpio
- Scorpio New Moon Intention
- Scorpio New Moon Healing Invocation

SCORPIO **Water** items: Essential Oils + Flower Essences

- Patchouli - detoxification
- Jasmine - sweetness
- Sandalwood - spirituality
- Ylang Ylang - balancing

SCORPIO NEW MOON NUMEROLOGY

There are many ways to incorporate numerology when formulating your ceremony. You can find numbers to work with in the degree of the sign, the date, the hour you conduct the ceremony, etc. The New Moon Numerology Empowerment Code is a special formula developed by Amanda Rieger Green, MPH at Wise Skies. We like to think of this as part of our secret sauce. We

use this number to find synchronicities as well as journaling on the day of the New Moon.

Scorpio New Moon Numerology Empowerment Code = 7

Numbers have power. We add the numbers that correlate with the Sun sign and the Moon sign, to create a unique code to use in ceremonies. During the New Moon, the Sun and the Moon appear in the same zodiac sign. That means each one is assigned the same number as the zodiac sign of Scorpio.

The Wise Skies Formula:
Scorpio Numerology Code = 8
Sun in Scorpio (8) + Moon in Scorpio (8) = 16
Reduce it to a single digit: 1+6 = 7

The "7" Empowerment Code promotes spiritual discovery, fact-finding, and seeking higher wisdom. Notice when you see a 7 today: it's a reminder that there's more to life than what meets the eye. Seeing a 7 reminds you to pause and consider a metaphoric meaning behind what is happening in the present moment. Connect the cosmic dots (mental, physical, emotional and spiritual) and you will likely emerge with a deeper, truer sense of Soul-awareness. It can enhance your ceremony to incorporate 7 of anything in your design.

Numerology Code Journaling

- *When do I find myself seeking and searching in order to deepen my spiritual journey?*
- *What are my spiritual disciplines?*
- *What do I love learning more about?*
- *Am I willing to dedicate time, energy and attention to my spiritual development in the energies of the Scorpio New Moon in order to create a richer, fuller day-to-day experience?*

SCORPIO NEW MOON CEREMONY
Enchanted Waters

The Scorpio New Moon enhances your connection with the Divine, while honing your supernatural, and intuitive abilities. This ceremony incorporates drumming and a natural body of Water to ignite your inner magician. Use this ceremony when you want to transcend, transform, and change any situation or mood.

BEFORE YOU BEGIN GATHERING TOOLS, SAY THE NEW MOON INVOCATION FOUND ON PAGE XX.

Step One: Selecting Tools

Set up a New Moon wishing area in a quiet space without distractions. Ideally you can do this outdoors, but a private space inside works too. Refer to the corresponding elements in the section above to select your tools. We suggest incorporating at least one tool per element (Fire, Earth, Air, Water), as well as a journal to write your intentions and responses to the journal prompts. You'll also need a drum, or makeshift instrument for this ceremony.

Step Two: Circle Up

For this ceremony, we prefer to be near a natural body of Water outside: lake, stream, river, ocean, or pond. A kiddie pool, bird bath, or bowl of Water in your backyard will work too. Outside, next to the Water, create a circle. You can do this with an assortment of crystals, candles (unlit), your journal, bottles of essential oils, etc. By using ceremony tools to create a circle, you are incorporating their energy (and your own) into the ceremony. Once you've created the circle, sit in the middle of it.

Step Three: Breath of Life

Sit up tall, finding length through the top of your head (your crown chakra) all the way down through the base of your spine (sacral chakra). Keeping your eyes open and with a fixed gaze in the distance, begin to notice your breath. Inhale deeply through your nose, filling your lungs with clean Air. When you exhale, open your mouth, stick out your tongue and let out a roar (and any bad vibes). In yoga, this is called the Lion's Breath. Repeat 7 times (purposely using the Scorpio Empowerment Code).

Say: *I breath life into this circle of eternal truth, wisdom and trust. There is no beginning and no end.*

Step Four: Activate

Light the candles. As you light each one . . .

Say: *I light the flame of eternity.*

Sprinkle a little of the essential oils around the circle clockwise.

Say: *I activate the eternal part of my senses.*

Put the essential oil bottle(s) back into their respective place in the circle.

With your right index finger, touch each crystal moving in a clockwise direction. With each one . . .

Say: *I activate the purest frequencies of light, energy, and intelligence.*

Step Five: Your Unique Rhythm

Pick up the drum or your instrument. Begin to create a hypnotic rhythm that streams from your heart, soul and the cosmos. Have fun with this. Relax and enjoy your own music. If you would like to sing or chant, feel free to embellish the music you are making in whatever way brings your unique life force to the circle and flows with the energy of the Scorpio New Moon.

Step Six: I AM

Remain seated in the middle of your circle and write out any New Moon intentions you wish to make. Reminder: the most optimal time to write intentions is within 8 hours of the exact time of the New Moon. You can write up to ten intentions. For this ceremony, write out at least three "I AM" intentions to chant.

I AM _____.

I AM _____.

I AM _____.

Step Seven: Pulse Sound into Being

Stand and take up the drum or your instrument of choice. Begin drumming or playing in an intuitive rhythm again. When you are ready, walk out of the circle. Speak your "I AM" mantras and wishes as you walk out of the circle toward the body of Water. If you can walk into or stand in the body of Water as you drum and chant your "I AM" mantras, this is ideal. If you cannot walk into the Water, stand beside it.

Allow the conductive powers of the Water to amplify your spoken wishes and intentions, as you create your unique song to the universe. Spend as much time chanting and drumming as you like. When you are finished, stand still in or next to the Water. Feel the vibrations of your body and the beat. Know that your actions have been seen and your words have been heard.

Imagine that you have roots extending from your feet into the ground. Envision that your roots permeate through to the core of the Earth where there is a giant quartz crystal. Visualize your roots attaching to that crystal. Breathe and feel yourself offering your intentions to the crystal core, to take intelligent root. Feel the vibrations of wishes granted coming back up through your body.

Say: I AM infinite. I AM a conscious co-creator of my reality. And so it is.

Step Eight: Closing Sacred Space

It is important to seal the energy after any ceremony. Refer to **page xx** for our suggestion on closing sacred space, or say your personalized closing prayers.

MAKING IT PERSONAL

Moon Musings

- Amanda

My action planets are in Scorpio - Mercury (communication and the processing of information), Mars (action and aggression), and Uranus (shock and awe). Needless to say, this is always an intense New Moon for me. I usually focus on how my actions are creating abundance or lack in my life experiences. It's a highly introspective Moon for me (very Scorpio). Here are a few musings from previous Scorpio New Moons:

- I process information and emotions with integrity, transparency and love to myself, to others. and to my Higher Power.
- I am safe in sharing information, ideas, creations, and inspiration in all relationships, groups, and environments.
- My psychic gifts and abilities are used only for the highest light, love, and intelligence in this lifetime. All darkness and lower vibrational energies are transmuted into pure light and love.
- I organically create time to quiet my mind, meditate, and interconnect with the infinite magic in and around me.

Best Wishes

- Tiffany

The New Moon in Scorpio hits in my 11th or 12th house depending on the degree of the New Moon. So sometimes I add elements relating to friends and wishes (11th house) or subconscious desires (12th house). My natal Sun, Moon, Mercury, and Uranus are all in Scorpio—so this is a particularly magnetizing birthday-Moon for me. Here are a few wishes I have used on previous Scorpio New Moons:

- I am selfless and powerful beyond measure in service to my highest divine vision.
- I am so grateful to be fulfilling God's mission for my life.
- I am one with my life's purpose, passions, and projects.
- I surrender other people to their own God-presence.
- I enjoy working with my galactic council to cause a wave of unconditional love and awakening through my business.
- I forgive quickly, and make amends whenever necessary, keeping my side of the street as clean as possible.
- I easily tap into the frequency of financial abundance.
- Above all, help me set aside what I think I know, and what I think I want, so that the Divine can flow through me. May I be of service to God and my fellows.

Sagittarius New Moon

WHEN THE NEW MOON IS IN SAGITTARIUS

When the New Moon falls in the Fire sign of Sagittarius, you can expect to feel spontaneous. You might notice extra playful energy, including some fun-loving, high-spirited vibes. This is the perfect Moon to plan a new adventure, to set an intention around exploring your connection with the Spiritual realm, or to overcome issues around excess. This is the Moon of the philosopher, the friend, and the gypsy. It's time to bang the drum of self-knowledge and look at the world with optimism.

Sagittarius is the ninth sign in the zodiac and is represented by the Centaur. It is a Fire sign, ruled by Jupiter.

Positive (High) Vibes of the Sagittarius New Moon

(*Make wishes in these areas*)
Travel and adventure
Higher education, students, and mentors
Involvement with artistic and multicultural endeavors
Truth-seeking, devotion and faith
Friends
Enthusiasm
Growth
Peace of mind and meditation
Ceremonies
Heirs and guardians
Abundance and fortune
Legal hearings/careers
Publishing books

Challenging (Low) Vibes of the Sagittarius New Moon

(*What you might wish to remove*)

Procrastination
Delusional thinking or overly optimistic attitudes

Over-doing things or exaggerating
Taking shortcuts
Making assumptions

In Health, Sagittarius Governs

(Areas of the body where you might wish for healing)

Hips
Thighs
Arteries
Liver
Sciatica
Solar Plexus (Manipura)

Sample Wishes for the New Moon in Sagittarius

- I easily find myself taking a trip to (insert place) with (insert people) at a price I can afford.
- I regularly reach out to my Higher Power to receive spiritual guidance and direction that I easily hear and trust.
- I successfully enroll in classes that assist me on my path in a fun and straightforward way.

Sagittarius New Moon Intention

I naturally embody freedom, peace, and joy each day and express my gratitude and contentment with no strings attached. True value happens in the present moment.

Sagittarius New Moon Healing Invocation

I invoke sacred healing space for evolutionary healing in my hips, thighs, arteries, liver and sciatica. My healing process is expanding my freedom and joy. I feel and express it in my body, mind, and spirit.

Word to the Wise

When the Moon is in Sagittarius, you are likely feeling energized and ready to get out of the house. Depending on your personal constituency and situation, you may enjoy the Fire energy. But if things are feeling too heated, you can incorporate elements from the opposite sign throughout the day to balance things out. The opposite sign of Sagittarius is the Air sign Gemini. Consider contemplative activities like a walking meditation in a labyrinth to combine action (Fire) with mindfulness (Air).

Working with Corresponding Elements

We suggest using one or more items of your choice from each element when designing your ceremony. Use as many or as few as you like.

SAGITTARIUS **Fire** items: Candles + Smoke

- Royal blue or purple candles - vision
- Floral scented candles, herbal bundles, or incense:
    - Sage - clearing
    - Lavender - calm
    - Rose - love

SAGITTARIUS **Earth** items: Crystals + Stones

- Peacock Ore - insight
- Lapis - creativity
- Green Aventurine - opportunity
- Lepidolite - meditation

SAGITTARIUS **Air** items: Intentions + Mantras

- Any personal wishes you want to make in the areas Sagittarius governs + the High Vibe Aspects of Sagittarius
- Sagittarius New Moon Intention
- Sagittarius New Moon Healing Invocation

SAGITTARIUS **Water** items: Essential Oils + Flower Essences

- Rosemary - passion
- Lavender - calm
- Eucalyptus - change
- Tea Tree - raising your vibration

SAGITTARIUS NEW MOON NUMEROLOGY

There are many ways to incorporate numerology when formulating your ceremony. You can find numbers to work with in the degree of the sign, the date, the hour you conduct the ceremony, etc. The New Moon Numerology Empowerment Code is a special formula developed by Amanda Rieger Green,

MPH at Wise Skies. We like to think of this as part of our secret sauce. We use this number to find synchronicities as well as journaling on the day of the New Moon.

Sagittarius New Moon Numerology Empowerment Code = 9

Numbers have power. We add the numbers that correlate with the Sun sign and the Moon sign, to create a unique code to use in ceremonies. During the New Moon, the Sun and the Moon appear in the same zodiac sign. That means each one is assigned the same number as the zodiac sign of Sagittarius.

The Wise Skies Formula:
Sagittarius Numerology Code = 9
Sun in Sagittarius (9) + Moon in Sagittarius (9) = 18
Reduce it to a single digit: 1+8 = 9

The "9" Empowerment Code promotes integrity, wisdom, and humanitarianism. Notice when you see a 9 today: it's a reminder to seek the path of integrity. By checking in with your true motives through rigorous honesty, you will find clarity. The path ahead may not be easy, however the reward will not only impact you wholly, its higher vibrations will reverberate throughout all humanity. Seeing a 9 reminds you to pause and take the high road and it will exponentially impact the greatest good of all. It can enhance your ceremony to incorporate 9 of anything in your design.

Numerology Code Journaling

- *When do I feel in integrity with my body, mind and spirit?*
- *In what area do I need to take the high road in my life?*
- *How can I draw upon my innate wisdom during this Sagittarius New Moon to give back to my community and leave my mark on the universe?*

SAGITTARIUS NEW MOON CEREMONY
Personal Altar

This personalized ceremony incorporates keepsakes and photos to ignite the magic of your unique spirit. This ceremony is ideal for creating your life's biggest adventure, increasing your worldview, and attracting new friends.

BEFORE YOU BEGIN GATHERING TOOLS, SAY THE NEW MOON INVOCATION FOUND ON PAGE XX.

Step One: Selecting Tools

Set up a New Moon wishing area in a quiet space without distractions. Ideally you can do this outdoors, but a private space inside works too. Refer to the corresponding elements in the section above to select your tools. We suggest incorporating at least one tool per element (Fire, Earth, Air, Water), as well as a journal to write your intentions and responses to the journal prompts.

Step Two: Preparing an Altar

Find a place at home that you can create a personal altar. This can be a small table, corner of a room, or anywhere you feel called to bless and honor as your personal and sacred space. Light a candle and place it in the center of your altar.

Say: This is the altar of my creation. I inspire this space with divine intelligence, love, and infinite abundance. May the flames of the Sagittarius New Moon purify this energy. Namaste.

Step Three: Clearing Space

Light some sage or an herbal bundle and smudge your body with smoke from head to toe three times. Next circle the altar clockwise 9 times (purposely using the Sagittarius Empowerment Code) with the smoke. Bring your palms together at your heart (prayer hands), bow to your own heart in front of your altar, giving thanks to your own divinity.

Step Four: Activating Crystal Magick

Creatively arrange your crystals in a grid around the edges of the altar. This activates the crystals to begin working with each other and incorporates sacred geometry. It's ideal to use at least three crystals for this space.

Starting with the crystal at the top of the altar (or northernmost point) and moving clockwise, touch each crystal with your right index finger.

Say: I activate a grid of light and sanctify this altar. My altar is a place of peace, love, and blessings, where my prayers are heard.

Repeat this with each crystal moving in a clockwise direction until you return to the first crystal.

Step Five: Making it Personal

Gather 9 personal items: pictures, figurines, an item of significance from a friend or loved-one, a special letter or card, jewelry, etc. Adding personal items that are special to you will focus your unique energy around your wishes. Choose what is speaking to you in the present moment. You can add more items later, but start with at least 3 in keeping with the frequency of creation.

Place the personal items on your altar. Dab a few drops of essential oil on your palms, then rub your palms together vigorously to create energy (you will feel the heat). When you are ready, hold your palms over your altar. Close your eyes.

Say: May the light of love and flame of eternity burn bright and bless this space.

Step Six: Set Intentions

Light a candle and put it on your altar while you think about what wishes and intentions you want to make. Pull inspiration and insights from your meditation and write up to 9 intentions in your journal. This is also an ideal time to write the New Moon Intention and the Healing Invocation. Reminder: the most potent time for wish-making is within eight hours of the New Moon. Once you have written out your intentions, place your journal on your altar for the next 9 nights. Prepare a place to sit still by the altar for a short meditation.

Step Seven: Visualize

Sit for a few minutes with your eyes closed. Visualize your main wish coming to fruition. How will it look when your intentions and wishes unfold? How will you feel? Where is it taking place? Be willing to have faith, and believe that your cosmic guidance team is supporting you in what is best for you at this time. Blow out the candle when you have completed the visualization.

Word to the Wise: This altar can be used for however long you like. You can add items, crystals and use it as a special place for meditation. Clear out the energy around it with a smudge stick every once in awhile. A good rule of thumb is to routinely clear the altar with each New and Full Moon. Know that your altar is a place where you can pray, honor teachers, remember loved ones, set intentions, or find solitude.

Step Eight: Closing Sacred Space

It is important to seal the energy after any ceremony. Refer to **page xx** for our suggestion on closing sacred space, or say your personalized closing prayers.

MAKING IT PERSONAL

Moon Musings
- Amanda

The Sagittarius New Moon is usually the last New Moon of the year. My natal Neptune is in Sagittarius and the Moon almost always hits my 6th house (vocation and health). It's a Moon where I combine work, health (6th house), open-mindedness and visionary thinking (Sagittarius). I usually reflect on the year and envision (Neptune) myself a year in the future. Here are a few Moon musings from previous Sagittarius New Moons:

- I recognize both healthy and unhealthy daily patterns of behavior, honoring what has been and how they have served me. I am willing to incorporate new daily routines that build upon healthy behaviors and organically let go of outmoded patterns.
- I experience a sense of fun, joy and spontaneity in my daily life, which naturally reinvigorates my spirits and created more vitality.
- I enjoy healthy friendships and friend-groups, attracting people who inspire unconditional attitudes and add greater freedom and abundance to my life, and vice versa.

- I emit unconditional love, joy and gratitude to Dennis (my husband) through my words, actions and energy-field. I am grateful for his ability to make me laugh and his caring heart.
- I clearly connect with my guides, other realms, dimensions, and beings in the highest light to aid in the divine alchemy of Earth and the multiverse. Higher levels of wisdom and intelligence are activated and naturally integrated within my DNA and cells.

Best Wishes

- Tiffany

The New Moon in Sagittarius hits in my 12th or 1st house depending on the degree of the New Moon. So, sometimes I add elements relating to subconscious desires (12th house) or ego/self (1st house). My natal Mars and Neptune are in Sagittarius—and I have Sag-rising. I usually experience extra energy and drive to pursue big dreams this time of year. Here are a few wishes I have used on previous Sagittarius New Moons:

- I experience life as a fun adventure.
- I have time to enjoy reading books on yogic philosophy.
- I love traveling and learning from new cultures while also balancing home, family, and work duties.
- I easily find ways to contribute positively to the family of humanity across the world.
- My biggest project of the year is unfolding organically and wisely.
- Above all, help me set aside what I think I know, and what I think I want, so that the Divine can flow through me. May I be of service to God and my fellows.

Capricorn New Moon

WHEN THE NEW MOON IS IN CAPRICORN

When the New Moon falls in the Earth sign of Capricorn, you can expect to feel ambitious, intuitive, and driven. This is the perfect Moon to set intentions around long-term plans and goals. This is the Moon of the purpose-driven leader. It's time to bang the drum of self-discipline and perhaps offer a renewed sense of commitment to something that requires slow and steady growth.

Capricorn is the tenth sign in the zodiac and is represented by the Sea-Goat. It is an Earth sign, ruled by Saturn.

Positive (High) Vibes of the Capricorn New Moon

(*Make wishes in these areas*)

Ambition and vision
Taking responsibility
Healing work
Discipline
Realistic, structured goals
Maturity and adulting
Traditions
Success and reputation
Long-term planning
Building your empire consciously and compassionately

Challenging (Low) Vibes of the Capricorn New Moon

(*What you might wish to remove*)

Rigidity and sternness
Resentment
Not staying in the present moment
Touchy or sensitive
Controlling tendencies

Pessimistic attitudes
Fear of change

In Health, Capricorn Governs

(Areas of the body where you might wish for healing)

Bones
Knees
Joints
Arthritis
Gall bladders
Skin
Root Chakra (Muladhara)
Crown Chakra (Sahasrara)

Sample Wishes for the New Moon in Capricorn

- I easily prepare for an early retirement and financial security.
- I am comfortable using my intuitive side in making business decisions.
- I refine my reputation and public image.

Capricorn New Moon Intention

I expand my light and perspective to include the bigger picture while trusting I am taking the right steps along my divine path. I experience fulfillment in the journey.

Capricorn New Moon Healing Invocation

I invoke sacred healing space and experience a complete and total healing in my bones, joints, and body structure. Health and well-being exudes from my skin with radiance, beauty and positivity as I trust my healing process, mind, body, and spirit.

Word to the Wise

When the Moon is in Capricorn, you are likely feeling ready to rise to any occasion. Depending on your personal constituency and situation, you may enjoy the stability and practicality that the Earth energy provides. But if things are feeling dense, fixed, or even stuck, you can incorporate elements from the opposite sign throughout the day to balance things out. The opposite sign of Capricorn is the Water sign Cancer. Consider Water-related activities to encourage fluidity: taking baths, drinking tea, making spritzes, using herbal sprays and tinctures, swimming in hot springs or a lake. It can be useful to combine the steadfastness of your intentions (Earth) with the flexibility of trusting providence to flow in at divine right timing (Water).

Working with Corresponding Elements

We suggest using one or more items of your choice from each element when designing your ceremony. Use as many or as few as you like.

CAPRICORN **Fire** items: Candles + Smoke

- Dark grey, black or deep red candles - trust
- Earthy scented candles, herbal bundles, or incense:
  - Palo Santo - protection
  - Sage - clarity
  - Patchouli - accelerated healing

CAPRICORN **Earth** items: Crystals + Stones

- Unakite Jasper - caring
- Garnet - passion
- Snowflake Obsidian - no strings attached
- Kambaba Jasper - higher wisdom
- Spirit Quartz - truth

CAPRICORN **Air** items: Intentions + Mantras

- Any personal wishes you want to make in the areas Capricorn governs + the High Vibe Aspects of Capricorn
- Capricorn New Moon Intention
- Capricorn New Moon Healing Invocation

CAPRICORN **Water** items: Essential Oils + Flower Essences

- Nutmeg - intellectual stimulation
- Juniper - processing
- Bergamot - letting go of fear

CAPRICORN NEW MOON NUMEROLOGY

There are many ways to incorporate numerology when formulating your ceremony. You can find numbers to work with in the degree of the sign, the date, the hour you conduct the ceremony, etc. The New Moon Numerology Empowerment Code is a special formula developed by Amanda Rieger Green, MPH at Wise Skies. We like to think of this as part of our secret sauce. We use this number to find synchronicities as well asmjournaling on the day of the New Moon.

Capricorn New Moon Numerology Empowerment Code = 2

Numbers have power. We add the numbers that correlate with the Sun sign and the Moon sign, to create a unique code to use in ceremonies. During the New Moon, the Sun and the Moon appear in the same zodiac sign. That means each one is assigned the same number as the zodiac sign of Capricorn.

The Wise Skies Formula:
Capricorn Numerology Code = 2
Sun in Capricorn (10) + Moon in Capricorn (10) = 20
Reduce it to a single digit: 2+0 = 2

The "2" Empowerment Code promotes partnerships, diplomacy, forgiveness, and trust. Notice when you see a 2 today: it's a reminder to connect consciously in relationships and to find balance. Seeing a 2 reminds you to pause and be fAir. It can enhance your ceremony to incorporate 2 of anything in your design.

Numerology Code Journaling

- *What does balanced connection feel like to me?*
- *How can I incorporate an interdependent attitude into all of my relationships and partnerships?*
- *In what areas of my life do I best practice diplomacy, objectivity, and fairness? Is there any forgiveness that I can initiate in the Capricorn New Moon energy in order to cultivate more peace and trust in my life?*

CAPRICORN NEW MOON CEREMONY

Pure Positive Potential

This ceremony uses crystal conductivity to pulse the frequency of your intentions and wishes into existence. Do this ceremony to magnify your ambitions, embrace responsibilities, and find excitement in long term goals.

BEFORE YOU BEGIN GATHERING TOOLS, SAY THE NEW MOON INVOCATION FOUND ON PAGE XX.

Step One: Selecting Tools

Set up a New Moon wishing area in a quiet space without distractions. Ideally you can do this outdoors, but a private space inside works too. Refer to the corresponding elements in the section above to select your tools. We suggest incorporating at least one tool per element (Fire, Earth, Air, Water), as well as a journal to write your intentions and responses to the journal prompts. You'll also need a glass of water and some note paper for this ceremony.

Step Two: Infuse Sacred Energy

Diffuse 2 (Capricorn Empowerment Code) drops of essential oils in your home and/or office space all month long starting on the day of the New Moon.

Step Three: Activate

Light a candle. If possible, leave it burning until it totally burns out. Within eight hours *after* the Capricorn New Moon, write your strongest desire on a small piece of paper. Tape the desire on a clear glass cup and fill with purified Water. Add 2 (Capricorn Empowerment Code) drops of ingestible essential oils and a clean crystal to the Water. Let it infuse for a few hours (outside if possible) while you work out and meditate on a power word. This is a great time to exert some physical energy (working out, doing yoga, cleaning your house). Focus on one strong desire. The Capricorn New Moon energy optimizes our ability to manifest our strongest goals, desires and dreams IF we have a clear vision and determination to see it and believe it.

Step Four: Conductivity

Make sure the essential oils you are using are safe to ingest. If not, you can pour the activated Water on your bare feet outside on the ground. Remove the crystal and then drink the infused Water, or pour it on your feet with gratitude. Word to the Wise: Water is a conductor. It takes on whatever energy, vibration, or words you are infusing it with.

Say: *I am activating divine determination, clear vision, and pure desire. As above, so below.*

Step Five: Write Intentions

Pull inspiration and insights from your desire, the word you focused on during your workout, the New Moon numerology (2), and the properties of Capricorn (as listed above in the areas Capricorn governs + the High Vibe Aspects of Capricorn) to write up to ten intentions in your journal. This is also an ideal time to write the New Moon Intention and the Healing Invocation.

Step Six: Visualize

Return to the lit candle. Visualize your main wish coming to fruition with your eyes softly gazing at the flame. How will it look when the intentions and wishes unfold? How will you feel? Where is it taking place? Be willing to have faith, and believe that your cosmic guidance team is supporting you in what is best for you at this time.

Say: *Thank you, Fire (extinguish your Fire and give a spiritual nod to the Earth, Wind, and Water elements, adding your own thoughts of gratitude).*

Step Seven: Closing Sacred Space

It is important to seal the energy after any ceremony. Refer to **page xx** for our suggestion on closing sacred space, or say your personalized closing prayers.

MAKING IT PERSONAL

Moon Musings
- Amanda

Capricorn New Moons are always a big "straighten up and fly right" kind of energy for me. I have Capricorn on both the cusps of my 6th (duties & responsibilities) and 7th (partnerships) houses. Because I'm a Libra, partnerships are already a big theme in my story in this lifetime, and this New Moon usually signifies new ways of being in my relationship with agendas and people. Here are some past musings from Capricorn New Moons:

- It is my intention to consciously transfer consciousness into my physical body and share upgraded vitality with others, each and every day.
- I see and experience my relationships with new levels of awareness, clarity, compassion, and reciprocity. I always check my motives for ego and selfishness in relationships.
- Any self-righteous or self-serving attitudes in partnerships are transmuted into compatibility, graciousness, and humility.
- I recognize and honor people with a genuine heart and tell them what they mean to me when it crosses my mind and heart. I give of my time and talents generously and with no strings attached.

Best Wishes
- Tiffany

The New Moon in Capricorn hits in my 1st or 2nd house depending on the degree of the New Moon. So, sometimes I add elements relating to ego/self (1st house) or values, money, and self-worth (2nd house). This Moon also squares my Libra planets: Jupiter, Saturn, Venus, and Pluto. Here are a few wishes I have used on previous Capricorn New Moons:

- I have enough self-discipline, ambition, competency, and motivation to responsibly lead my team.
- I welcome the removal of all sternness, impatience, inflexibility, and defects of character in my mind and heart.
- I age gracefully, becoming stronger and more agile the older I get.
- The right ideas occur to me to generate useful content and make maximum impact.

- I study with the best teachers on my path to set me up with deep understanding and long-term success.
- I gladly receive recognition for a job well done and feel that my work has made a significant impact.
- Life gets better and better.
- Above all, help me set aside what I think I know, and what I think I want, so that the Divine can flow through me. May I be of service to God and my fellows.

Aquarius New Moon

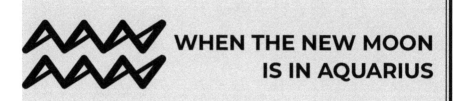

WHEN THE NEW MOON IS IN AQUARIUS

When the New Moon falls in the Air sign of Aquarius, you can expect some sparks to fly. You might notice extra energy and advantageous personality quirks. This is the perfect Moon to tap into your inner Einstein, set a new intention to live in the collective consciousness, or try something new. This is the Moon of the inventor and the free spirit. It's time to bang the drum of self-renewal and look at the world with fresh eyes.

Aquarius is the eleventh sign in the zodiac and is represented by the Water Bearer. It is an Air sign, ruled by Saturn and Uranus.

Positive (High) Vibes of the Aquarius New Moon

(*Make wishes in these areas*)

Empowering groups
Human rights
Out of the box thinking
Futuristic inventions
Curiosity and innovation
Networking
Being honest with yourself and others

Challenging (Low) Vibes of the Aquarius New Moon

(*What you might wish to remove*)

Being overwhelmed
Aloof behavior
Self-righteousness
Being flakey
Judgmental attitudes

In Health, Aquarius Governs

(*Areas of the body where you might wish for healing*)

Circulation
Legs
Ankles
Heart Chakra (Anahata)
Crown Chakra (Sahasrara)

Sample Wishes for the New Moon in Aquarius

- I easily find my self initiating creative solutions.
- I love finding new groups of like-minded people.
- I enjoy being involved with activism to help the greater good.

Aquarius New Moon Intention

I surround myself with inspirational people and recognize the extraordinary in the ordinary.

Aquarius New Moon Healing Invocation

I invoke sacred healing space for overall well-being and vitality in my legs and ankles. My circulatory system functions optimally, adding not only health but the life pulse of divine intelligence into my being. I know I am worthy of a healthy body.

Word to the Wise

When the Moon is in Aquarius, it's possible you are feeling pulled in many directions. Depending on your personal constituency and situation, you may enjoy the endless options provided under an Air-Moon. But if things are feeling too indecisive and scattered, you can incorporate elements from the opposite sign throughout the day to balance things out. The opposite sign of Aquarius is Leo. Consider contemplative yoga or something that combines thought (Air) with action (Fire).

Working with Corresponding Elements

We suggest using one or more items of your choice from each element when designing your ceremony. Use as many or as few as you like.

AQUARIUS **Fire** items: Candles + Smoke

- Aqua or Teal Candles - clarity
- Herbal scented candles, herbal bundles, or incense:

- Rosemary (dried bundle) - passion
- Lavender - serenity

AQUARIUS **Earth** items: Crystals + Stones

- Labradorite - transformation
- Chrysoprase - attracting abundance
- Botswana Agate - soothing
- Blue Calcite - mental clarity

AQUARIUS **Air** items: Intentions + Mantras

- Any personal wishes you want to make in the areas Aquarius governs + the High Vibe Aspects of Aquarius
- Aquarius New Moon Intention
- Aquarius New Moon Healing Invocation

AQUARIUS **Water** items: Essential Oils + Flower Essences

- Cypress - spiritual grounding
- Ginger - anti-stress
- Coriander - processing
- Lavender - calming

AQUARIUS NEW MOON NUMEROLOGY

There are many ways to incorporate numerology when formulating your ceremony. You can find numbers to work with in the degree of the sign, the date, the hour you conduct the ceremony, etc. The New Moon Numerology Empowerment Code is a special formula developed by Amanda Rieger Green, MPH at Wise Skies. We like to think of this as part of our secret sauce. We use this number to find synchronicities as well as journaling on the day of the New Moon.

Aquarius New Moon Numerology Empowerment Code = 22

Numbers have power. We add the numbers that correlate with the Sun sign and the Moon sign, to create a unique code to use in ceremonies. During the New Moon, the Sun and the Moon appear in the same zodiac sign. That means each one is assigned the same number as the zodiac sign of Aries.

The Wise Skies Formula:
Aquarius Numerology Code = 11

Sun in Aquarius (11) + Moon in Aquarius (11) = 22

Normally we reduce a two-digit number to a single digit by adding the two numbers together. We intentionally *don't* do that with an 11, 22, or 33 because they are considered Master Numbers. Master Numbers offer us a double dose of energy, lessons, opportunities and magical powers to tap into deeper wisdom and innate abundance. With these Master Numbers we get to work with both the base vibration (2 + 2 = 4) and the master vibration (22).

The "22" Empowerment Code assists with turning dreams into reality, and building foundations that last. Notice when you see a 22 today: it's a reminder to be present in your thoughts, as they, along with your emotions are manifesting your reality. Seeing a 22 reminds you to pause and think about the highest version of what you really want and believe you are worthy of receiving it. To enhance your ceremony, incorporate **4** of anything in your design (reducing the 22 to 2+2 = 4).

Numerology Code Journaling

- *What dreams and desires am I willing to express?*
- *Do I believe these dreams will become reality?*
- *What beliefs do I need to articulate around my dreams and desires to take action in this Aquarius New Moon energy for a bigger, more fulfilling, and abundant future?*

AQUARIUS NEW MOON CEREMONY
Raise the Vibe of the Tribe

This ceremony uses the power of the mind to ignite change in the collective conscience. If you want to make a difference, you can. This ceremony sparks change both in your personal life and in the world around you. We are stronger together.

BEFORE YOU BEGIN GATHERING TOOLS, SAY THE NEW MOON INVOCATION FOUND ON PAGE XX.

Step One: Selecting Tools

Set up a New Moon wishing area in a quiet space without distractions. Ideally you can do this outdoors, but a private space inside works too. Refer to the corresponding elements in the section above to select your tools. We suggest incorporating at least one tool per element (Fire, Earth, Air, Water), as well as a journal to write your intentions and responses to the journal prompts. You'll also need a recent newspaper, a blue marker, and a fire pit or safe place inside to burn things, such as a large metal bowl over a sink.

Step Two: Ignite the Light

Begin by lighting a Fire in your Fire pit, Fireplace, or Firebowl, wherever it is safe for you to burn paper. An outdoor grill can also work. Next, light one or more candles. Keep them safely next to you for the ceremony. Place crystals around the Fire pit to activate a sanctuary of transformation.

Say: *I light the eternal flame of the collective consciousness. I tap into the genius mind of Aquarian energy. All aspects of me are here now—Past, Present and Future. I open the multiverse.*

Step Three: Sparks Fly

Carefully, drop 4 drops of your chosen essential oil(s) into the Fire. Next, dab a drop of oil on your right index finger, rub it 4 times clockwise on the crown of your head (crown chakra). Repeat this on your third eye (on your forehead, in between your eyebrows), on your throat and on the back of your neck.

Step Four: Centered in the Flames

Dab a little more of the essential oil(s) on your palms. Rub them together briskly 4 times. Hold your palms at a safe distance over the Fire pit. Close your eyes and breath deeply in and out. Once you feel grounded, it's time to open your eyes and start writing. Using the intentions, Numerology, journal prompts, and whatever is on your mind, write for 4 to 22 minutes.

Step Five: Raise the Vibration

Once you've finished journaling, get the newspaper. Flip through it. Wherever you see anything negative, sad, provoking, or disheartening, take your blue marker and circle it. In the center of the circle . . .

Write: *More Love. Never Less.*

Repeat this throughout the paper. Each time you write "More Love. Never Less." breathe in and out deeply, feeling more love in your heart, and abundantly and unconditionally sending it out to the collective consciousness.

Step Six: Empower the Powerful

Next, go through the paper, and where you see "good news," acts of kindness, heartwarming stories, joyful celebrations, and recognition, draw a heart around all good news with your blue marker. Repeat this action for each piece of uplifting of information, magnifying these with the power of your love, and with joy and celebration sending each one out to the collective consciousness..

Step Seven: Transmute

Write out your Aquarius-themed wishes on the newspaper. This is also a good time to write out your Aquarius New Moon Intention and Healing Invocation as well. Reminder: this should be done within the first 8 hours of the New Moon. When you are ready, crumple each sheet of newspaper, and carefully burn it in the Fire, one sheet at a time. For each sheet . . .

Say: *I ignite more love and send it into the collective consciousness. I send this transmuted energy out into the cosmos to effect change, love and peace. I am empowered through the unconditional service of my heart to ignite light and love in the world.*

Step Eight: Recenter Yourself in the Flames

Once you have finished, repeat Step Four, dabbing essential oil on your palms, rubbing them together and holding your hands over the flame.

Say: *May the magic of the Moon stir the souls of the masses into selfless service. We are raising the vibration together.*

Step Nine: Closing Sacred Space

It is important to seal the energy after any ceremony. Refer to **page xx** for our suggestion on closing sacred space, or say your personalized closing prayers.

Step Ten: Continued Activation

When you are ready, take your candle with you, or you can leave it by the Fire, but allow it to safely burn all the way out. Gather the crystals and sleep with them under your pillow for the next 4 nights. Journal about any dreams or visions you have over the next 4 nights. Share your experiences and intuitive ideas triggered in the ceremony. In the coming weeks—notice any healing or change in the topics you circled and blessed on the newspaper. Have the headlines changed?

MAKING IT PERSONAL

Moon Musings
- Amanda

My South Node of the Moon is in Aquarius. I often find familiarity (both presently and karmically) in Aquarius-minded attitudes and behaviors, both high vibes and low vibes. This energy always triggers an opportunity to use my Aquarian genius-mind in more practical and less detached ways. Here are a few musings from previous Aquarius New Moons:

- I connect with my genius mind in this lifetime—and lifetime past and future—and willingly and easily share thoughts with others.
- I relate to those around me and know that my vulnerability builds trust.
- When isolating and detached tendencies surface, I recognize them and realize that these tendencies are no longer in my reality. I am

safe and free to exist and vibrate at a frequency of authenticity and genuine trust.

- The collective is awake, aware and seeing reality as it is with a discerning eye, genuine heart, and sense of empowerment. We change the world. We create a reality and consciousness of love.

Best Wishes

- Tiffany

The New Moon in Aquarius hits in my 2nd or 3rd house depending on the degree of the New Moon. So, sometimes I add elements relating to money and self-worth (2nd house) or communications and writing (3rd house). This Moon squares all of my Scorpio-planets: Mercury, Moon, Sun, and Uranus. Here are a few wishes I have used on previous Aquarius New Moons:

- I easily find myself aligning with my Destiny with clarity.
- I easily begin developing an app that has broad appeal and is useful to a large number of people.
- I experience life as revitalizing, with happy surprises and revelations.
- I invoke brilliant, inventive solutions quickly and easily all year.
- I easily tap into the manifestation magic of dreams coming true.
- Above all, help me set aside what I think I know, and what I think I want, so that the Divine can flow through me. May I be of service to God and my fellows.

Pisces New Moon

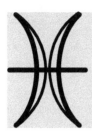

WHEN THE NEW MOON IS IN PISCES

When the New Moon falls in the Water sign of Pisces, you can expect to experience heightened empathy. You might notice yourself feeling more teary and compassionate than usual. This is the perfect Moon to initiate a charitable project, to start new lessons in the arts or music, or increase your spiritual gifts. This is the Moon of the Mystic and the Giver. It's time to bang the drum of self-assurance and look at the world with kindness.

Pisces is the twelfth sign in the zodiac and is represented by two Fish. It is a Water sign, ruled by Jupiter and Neptune.

Positive (High) Vibes of the Pisces New Moon

(*Make wishes in these areas*)

Compassion
Charity
Intuition
Artistic abilities
Healthy boundaries
Mystical reading lists
Meditation and mindfulness practices
Strategic giving and volunteerism (budgeting time and money)

Challenging (Low) Vibes of the Pisces New Moon

(*What you might wish to remove*)

Taking on too much
Toxic environments
Unhealthy boundaries (or lack thereof)
Depression or sadness
Escapism
Addiction
Delusional thinking

In Health, Pisces Governs

(Areas of the body where you might wish for healing)

Feet and toes
Lymphatic system
Sacral Chakra (Svadhisthana)
Solar Plexus (Manipura)

Sample Wishes for the New Moon in Pisces

- I easily find myself in the right place at the right time.
- I trust my intuition to know when to say yes and when to say no.
- I easily start a new meditation practice to clear my mind.

Pisces New Moon Intention

I create space for mindful and heartfelt interactions organically, without conditions or strings attached.

Pisces medicine healing invocation

I invoke sacred healing space from the tips of my toes and bottoms of my feet up through my entire body, lymphatic system and the cosmos. I am divine healing. My heart-centered consciousness heals my inner self and the universe. I transcend lower vibrational energies with divine compassion.

Word to the Wise

When the Moon is in Pisces it's possible you are feeling heightened emotions, increased intuition, and more empathy. Depending on your personal constituency and situation, you may enjoy the emotional depth provided under a Water-Moon. But if things are feeling too heavy, you can incorporate elements from the opposite sign throughout the day to balance things out. The opposite sign of Pisces is Virgo. Consider drumming, gardening, walking on the ground outside with bare feet, or visualizing roots growing from your feet to the center of the Earth in meditation to combine emotions (Water) with stability and practical outcomes (Earth). Combining Water and Earth elements assists you in anchoring your intentions with practical action.

Working with Corresponding Elements

We suggest using one or more items of your choice from each element when designing your ceremony. Use as many or as few as you like.

PISCES **Fire** items: Candles + Smoke

- Indigo, deep blue, purple or violet candles - dreaming
- Ancient scented candles, herbal bundles, or incense:
    - Sandalwood - spiritual grounding
    - Frankincense - consciousness

PISCES **Earth** items: Crystals + Stones

- Blue Lace Agate - auric clearing
- Goldstone - grounded spirituality
- Citrine - clarity
- Smokey Quartz - sustainability

PISCES **Air** items: Intentions + Mantras

- Any personal wishes you want to make in the areas Pisces governs + the High Vibe Aspects of Pisces
- Pisces New Moon Intention
- Pisces New Moon Healing Invocation

PISCES **Water** items: Essential Oils + Flower Essences

- Sandalwood - spiritual grounding
- Cedarwood - connectivity
- Elemi - mental calming
- Peppermint - excitement

PISCES NEW MOON NUMEROLOGY

There are many ways to incorporate numerology when formulating your ceremony. You can find numbers to work with in the degree of the sign, the date, the hour you conduct the ceremony, etc. The New Moon Numerology Empowerment Code is a special formula developed by Amanda Rieger Green, MPH at Wise Skies. We like to think of this as part of our secret sauce. We use this number to find synchronicities as well as journaling on the day of the New Moon.

Pisces New Moon Numerology Empowerment Code = 6

Numbers have power. We add the numbers that correlate with the Sun sign and the Moon sign, to create a unique code to use in ceremonies. During the New Moon, the Sun and the Moon appear in the same zodiac sign. That means each one is assigned the same number as the zodiac sign of Pisces.

The Wise Skies Formula:
Pisces Numerology Code = 12
Sun in Pisces (12) + Moon in Pisces (12) = 24
Reduce it down to a single digit: 2+4 = 6

The "6" Empowerment Code promotes unconditional love, peace, and nurturing. Notice when you see a 6 today: it's a reminder to stay connected and to find balance. Seeing a 6 reminds you to pause and be kind. It can enhance your ceremony to incorporate 6 of anything in your design.

Numerology Code Journaling

- *When do I practice unconditional love with both myself and others?*
- *How can nurture myself and others during the Pisces New Moon?*
- *How can I create more peace and love in all aspects of my life?*

PISCES NEW MOON CEREMONY

Dreams Come True

This ceremony uses the conductivity of Water to help you shift into higher levels of consciousness and greater awareness. You can use this ceremony anytime for healing and increasing your compassion.

BEFORE YOU BEGIN GATHERING TOOLS, SAY THE NEW MOON INVOCATION FOUND ON PAGE XX.

Step One: Selecting Tools

Set up a New Moon wishing area in a quiet space without distractions. Ideally you can do this outdoors, but a private space inside works too. Refer to the corresponding elements in the section above to select your tools. We suggest incorporating at least one tool per element (Fire, Earth, Air, Water), as well as a journal to write your intentions and responses to the journal prompts. You'll also need some meditation music and a glass pitcher of purified water for this ceremony.

Step Two: Ignite the Light

As you light the candle . . .

Say: *I am lighting the flame of clarity, compassion and eternal oneness. This space is sacred. This space is pure love. (Repeat three times to call in the frequency of creation, or repeat **6** times to invoke the Pisces Empowerment Code.)*

Step Three: Oils & Ahas

Turn on some meditation music. Dab a drop of essential oil on your index finger, then rub it clockwise in 6 circles on the crown of your head. Next rub the oil clockwise 6 times on your third eye. Repeat this on your throat, back of your neck, and breastbone. Breathe.

Write about what you are feeling, dreaming, and wanting to call into your life at this time. Use the Pisces astrology and numerology prompts above to guide you.

Step Four: Set Intentions

When you are finished journaling, gather one or more crystals and wash them to make sure they are clean. Place the crystal(s) in your glass pitcher filled with purified Water. While the Water is attuning to the frequency of each crystal, write 6 (or more) intentions using the properties of Pisces as listed above in the areas Pisces governs + the High Vibe Aspects of Pisces. This is also an ideal time to write the New Moon Intention and the Healing Invocation. Reminder: the most potent time for wish-making is within eight hours of the New Moon.

Step Five: Magic Moon Water

Meditate on the intentions you have written and discern the one that is ascendant or primary—the one that appears to have more energy than the rest. Write out the intention again on a small piece of paper and tape the paper on the outside of the glass pitcher, ink side facing in.

Say: *May the healing frequencies of the crystals fully infuse this Water with the essence of my intention. I trust the magic of the process. And so it is.*

Step Six: Visualize

Place the glass pitcher of Water outside for a few hours. Sit in a meditative posture that is comfortable for you, with a straight back, take a few cleansing breaths, and visualize your intention playing out. How would it feel if your intention was manifesting? Tap into the feeling tone as deeply as possible for 6 minutes, noticing your breath. Then, remove the crystal(s) and drink a full glass of the energy-infused Water.

*Option: Instead of drinking the Water, consider stepping into a shower or tub and pouring it along your spine starting at the base of your skull.

Step Seven: Closing Sacred Space

It is important to seal the energy after any ceremony. Refer to **page xx** for our suggestion on closing sacred space, or say your personalized closing prayers.

Extra credit: Read *The Hidden Messages in Water* by Dr. Masuru Emoto for a deeper understanding of how you can work with Water magic and intentions.

MAKING IT PERSONAL

Moon Musings

- Amanda

Pisces New Moons are always about higher calling, seeking, and searching out who I am in the world. For the last few years, during the PIsces New Moon, I've been on a yoga retreat in Costa Rica with my sister. We spend the New Moon in a ceremony that I am honored to facilitate each year. It is a beautifully heart-centered, vulnerable and activating time for me. This energy holds a sacred space place card in my heart and soul.

- I lead with love. I breathe with beauty. I give with purity. I exist with serenity.
- My voice and energy transmit high vibrational healing and reconnection to source-consciousness. I hold sacred space with peace and truth.
- I feel blessings and bliss flow through my body like waves on the ocean.
- My higher self and oversoul collaborate with the highest vibrational forces in the cosmos to become more loving, giving, and conscious.
- Time expands with each breath of trust, presence, and truth. We are one.
- Presence and inspiration flows from my being in a sustainable way that aligns with my work in the world. I am exactly where I am supposed to be. My work is my mission. I am in integrity with every aspect of my being.
- Being in tune with my dreams and desires flows naturally and practically.

Best Wishes

- Tiffany

I love incorporating water into my wishing ceremonies. I had the good fortune to meet Dr. Masuru Emoto before his death. Dr. Emoto's book, *The Hidden Messages in Water*, illustrates how much our consciousness affects water and everything around us. Fulfillment of wishes starts with the mood. Behind the mood is the intention. The New Moon in Pisces hits in my 3rd or 4th house depending on the degree of the New Moon. So, sometimes I add elements relating to writing and communications (3rd house) or home and family (4th house). Here are a few wishes I have used on previous Pisces New Moons:

- I easily deal with chaos and confusion in a constructive way that generates compassion and kindness.
- My imagination and dreams offer clarity and practical insights to my questions.
- I enjoy feeling part of the Universal flow of Love.
- I regularly feel connection with my Spirit Team.
- I find myself being more tolerant, patient, and accepting of people, knowing we are all one.
- Above all, help me set aside what I think I know, and what I think I want, so that the Divine can flow through me. May I be of service to God and my fellows.

"Rituals are like electrically powered transmitters sending stimulating sparks of electric current or inspirational feelings that connect us to our inner being or soul."

— *Wes Adamson, Imagination by Moonlight*

PART 3

Full Moon Ceremonies

Friendly reminder: If you're new to this, you may be thinking: "I'm an Aries!" and have fun identifying with some of the major Aries themes. However, we ALL live under the Aries New/Full Moon when it's high in the sky, and we can ALL take advantage of creating ceremony for an Aries Moon, no matter what our astrological birth sign. That is to say, the ceremonies in this book are not specific to your horoscope sign. They are specific to what is going on *in the Sky*.

Yes, you will need to know what sign the Moon is in to best use the ceremonies in this book. But you don't have to worry—there are free resources online to help you find what phase and sign the Moon is in. Once you know those two items, you're ready to use the ceremonies in this book.

Full Moon Ceremonies

"A ritual serves a bridge to carry purposeful, symbolic meaning to the personal or collective conscious and subconscious mind. When consciously created and enacted, ritual can be transforming; linking the past, present, and future into a continuum that can be observed, felt, and learned from."

- Ruth Barrett, *Women's Rites, Women's Mysteries*

The Full Moon is a lunar power time symbolizing wisdom and enchantment.

The Moon does not shine on it's own, rather it reflects the light of the Sun. At this time, we become open to reflecting on the previous cycles so that we can find completion with common issues and/or karmic patterns.

The Full Moon phase is an ideal time to receive divine blessings and insights for personal and spiritual growth. These lunar vibrations activate energy for finding practical solutions, ending patterns, and finding a sense of closure.

During the Full Moon, we perform ceremonies to illuminate what we need to know about divine will in our life. We ask ourselves and Spirit: What is the next right step? We can make wishes and set intentions not only for ourselves but also to raise the energy of the collective consciousness here on Earth.

Reminder: it takes time for wishes to manifest. The Universe is co-creating with you at it's own pace, weaving things together that are in your best interest, according to your unique needs and desires. Unanswered wishes are not mistakes.

Full Moon Ceremony Suggestions

We offer ideas for ceremonies based on what we like to do, but the beauty of creating your own ceremony is that you get to intuitively make the rules. There is no right or wrong. Your motive, intentions, and humble connection to Spirit is what matters most.

We offer three core suggestions for your Full Moon ceremonies:

(1) Conduct your ceremony and write wishes within the first few hours of the Full Moon - this is the most astrologically potent time.

(2) Use at least one of the recommended tools from each of the elements listed below in step one, but you can use as many or as few as you like.

(3) Enjoy yourself—don't take things too seriously. These ceremonies are intended to be a fun way for you to co-create the life of your dreams while honing your connection with the divine realm.

Full Moon Invocation

Full Moon invocations are opening dialogues or prayers with Spirit Guides. Some of us speak directly to God. Others speak to the personified energy of the Full Moon and its innate intelligence. In this way, we can honor the Moon as a physical manifestation of God energy in this world.

In whatever way you wish to view it, the Full Moon invocation is a time of alignment with the divine force to ask for light to be shed on what has been lurking in the shadows of your life, and to transmute energy-limiting blocks into limitless energy abundance.

This invocation also offers an opportunity to open and create sacred space. It is an invitation for the highest love and intelligence to be with you and support you throughout the ceremony.

Opening Sacred Space

Suggested for you to open sacred space for each Full Moon ceremony.

Say: *I open this sacred space—calling in the highest love, light, and divine intelligence—and align it with the purest energies of my mind, body and spirit. I am the housekeeper of my universe, clearing any lower vibrational energies that have been blocking the divine flow of pure, positive potential.*

I trust the precision of universal flow. I honor those who came before and those who will come after me. We are one.

Everything that is created is never destroyed, only transformed.

As above, so below.

I am the cosmic eraser, cleanser, and transformer. May the Full Moon in
_____ *(zodiac sign) illuminate dense and stagnant energies and transmute them into abundance. I invoke the highest energies of the* _____ *(zodiac sign) Full Moon in love, in light, and in divine intelligence.*

And so it is.

Closing Sacred Space

The below is our suggestion for you to close sacred space for each Full Moon ceremony.

After the ceremony is complete, bring your palms together in front of your heart or your forehead (third eye). Close your eyes and take three breaths, breathing in and out through your nose.

Visualize a channel of white liquid light flowing through the crown of your head, down through your spine, and then down into the Earth to clear your physical, emotional, and spiritual body. Visualize this light becoming fluorescent in cleansing your DNA and the cells of your body, and then shining it's unique rays out from your heart into the world.

Say: *I honor myself, this sacred space, and the divine intelligence guiding my life. I trust my Higher Power to overlight my intentions and to align my heart with the highest good of the collective. This ceremony is whole and complete. I give thanks, it is done, and so it is. Namaste.*

With hands in prayer, bow to the inner divinity of your own sacred heart, honoring your highest self. Remember God with gratitude.

Journey Into the Unknown: Full Moon in Mayan Territory

Amanda relates her experience moving from Texas to Belize.

The Full Moon is recognized as a time of closure, but something different happened on my first Moon in Belize. I journaled the whole experience of moving to Belize. The story is about walking the path of wonder and mystery.

June 26, 2019: Times are Changing

My husband Dennis began his trek to our new home in Belize five days ago. He's been driving from Texas through Mexico with Tex's new baby sister Abby, two of his rough and tough guy friends, a boat, and an attitude of adventure. From our intermittent texts and his Facebook chronology, they are having a trip to remember. Meanwhile, I've had the big dog on a weight-loss plan and have spent some quality time with my mom, who is as excited for me as she is terrified for the changes we're both facing.

July, 1 2019: Journey to a New Land

The day is here. I'm officially moving to Belize for real on the eve of the Cancer Solar Eclipse. I love how the nurturing energies of Cancer are divinely supporting this journey. It's truly an odd feeling after five years—preparing to uproot your entire life, forsaking every creature comfort, and leaving behind the security of home and routine—and the day actually *arrives*. I've got my 12-year old labrador Tex with me. He had to lose 9 pounds to meet the weight requirements for an in-cabin flight as my emotional support dog for the plane.

I say emotional support dog loosely because it's quite the opposite. I'm his emotional support human.

Mom drops Tex and me off at the Airport with my one piece of luggage, and we share a final hug goodbye. I love and admire my mom. She's been my rock over the last few months in the crunch time of the move, liquidating our household, and determining what goes on a freighter to ship over. She's helped me navigate the emotional carnival of juggling life and work and leaving everything familiar. And through it all, Mom is walking gracefully through terminal cancer. She isn't battling it, she is walking through it. And she is managing it all with honesty, integrity and presence.

She finally says, "I love you honey. I'm so excited for you and Dennis. Take care of my boy (Tex). I'll see you soon."

"I love you, too. Thank you, Mom."

And that's it.

I'm not going to cry, but I'm a little teary as the plane rolls down the tarmac, and yet Tex is making himself comfortable under a little boy's seat next to me. Tex is right at home and we aren't even there yet. His home is me. I think of that as the plane roars into the Air and we embark on this new adventure together.

July 4, 2019: Not a National Holiday in Belize

We are in Belize, in our new (old) home on high ground in a small village on the Sittee River. This home was originally a Seventh-Day Adventist Church. It's concrete and wood. It wasn't until a British couple moved in and made renovations and additions that it took on it's breezy, British Colonial Carribean style. mahogany, teak, and other hardwoods are stunning and will be restored in all their glory once we are finished. The Sittee is deep, twenty feet deep in most parts but 60 to 70 feet deep where we are. Too deep to build a dock in front of the house. Darrin, our contractor (and also the town Mayor), knows this because his stepfather used to free-dive here. This is where the Water is deepest—and it's also where the hidden treasure is. Literally.

July 5, 2019: Dead trees

There are three dead trees on our property and a few more trees that, if hit with a big storm, could easily come crashing down on the house. First order of business: Darrin's crew removes the trees. The trees are intense, especially the one outside the bathroom window. It's got snake-like cactus vines overtaking it, as if the life is being strangled out of it. Darrin, Dennis and I are standing together as the massive crane powers through the jungle, clearing a new path to extract the trees. Darrin laughs and says, "You know, Ms. Nadja (the British woman who lived here for nearly 28 years before us) used to bring snakes to the property and let them loose right back there." He points to the snake-strangler tree. We all just look at each other and then back at the tree.

July 7, 2019: Disturbance

After the removal of the dead trees, the energy completely shifted from light to dark. It feels ominous and heavy. I feel like I am walking through quicksand in paradise. My outlook is positive, motivated, and excited for the thrills of the day, yet my auric field feels cloudy and blurry. I'm doing my usual ceremonies and magic with an assortment of crystals, sage, epsom salts and more, but nothing is clearing me. I can't shake it on my own.

July 8, 2019: Hives and caves

On to the next order of business: hives and caves. Bees and bats. The animal medicine was calling. Out on the screened in porch overlooking the river, there is a massive swarm of africanized bees living in a hive in the right hand corner of the ceiling. As the bees buzz on the porch, it's an odd thing to realize there are possibly over one hundred thousand of them—yet they don't bother us. The make their presence known with their buzzing and busyness, but they are not interfering with our space. And, we knew when we bought the property that the dilapidated building in the back corner would eventually become my office. It's a total bat sanctuary. One day their cave will be my cave.

Unfortunately, colonies of bats and bees are unsafe and degrade the integrity of the house. Darrin sent off for the resident village bee expert, Mr. Gregory, and we turned our attention to the bats.

July 8, 2019 (part 2): Bat Medicine = Rebirth

What we didn't know was that there was also a community of bats living in the ceiling of the house. That became quite apparent when we woke up the first morning with little black droppings all over the light grey sheets. We decided to relocate ourselves downstairs asap until we could find the bats another home. Funny enough, in my one suitcase I had packed two oracle decks—my tried-and-true, and my spirit animal. I knew these would come in handy. I immediately went to my spirit animal oracle deck and pulled the bat card.

Bat: "A rebirth is assured. For the very best elements of what you had to give up in the death of old are still present in this new, amazing life forming now."

—*The Spirit Animal Oracle*, Colette Baron-Reid

In ancient Mayan culture, bats were not only part of the ceremony, they were actually part of the revered Mayan Calendar. The caves where bats hang out were believed to be part of the sacred underworld. So, naturally, bats were regarded as the messengers of the underworld, much the same as hawks in the Native American totem are regarded as messengers of the gods. The Mayan bat god, Camazotz, was included and summoned in ceremony, especially in death rites and rituals. Bats were also closely linked to human sacrifice, which was a common practice in the Mayan culture.

July 9, 2019: Bee Charmer

Darrin shows up with Mr. Gregory around 8:00pm—after the sun has set. Mr. Gregory is an older gentleman, originally from Honduras, who relocated here after he served in the military as a young man, and he stands tall with a quiet yet wise presence. He gears up in his bee suit and flip flops. Darrin, Dennis and I are quietly amused as we watch him climb up the ladder to inspect the hive. He begins removing boards and says, "There are two hives, and two queens. Hmmm. Unusual this close together."

And, so it begins. Like some bee whisperer from the jungle, Mr. Gregory, the bee charmer, begins gently removing the hive. Both Dennis and Darrin are twitching like scared little kids during the whole process, and both of them are getting stung a few times as they try to help Mr. Gregory with the flashlight and buckets for the honeycombs. All the while, not one sting for Mr. Gregory as he pulls out boards and bees swarm. Finally I say, "Y'all get out of here. I'll help him." Earth mother kicks in.

Two huge mop buckets of honeycomb. And it's like nothing I've seen or tasted. It has a sweet and almost salty tang as I lick it off my fingers. The only sting I get is on the elbow as I reached into one of the buckets and offended the last bee coming out of a comb. I laughed, but it throbbed for three days—a constant reminder of bee energy.

In ancient Mayan culture bees were sacred for bringing life to pollinate the Earth. If they accidently killed a bee, they would burn it. The *Melipona Yucateca*—a stingless bee native to Central America—was revered not only for it's gentle nature but for the healing and spiritual properties of its honey.

July 10, 2019: Rite of Passage

I can feel the metaphorical sacrifice and rebirth in my bones, and a deep connection to the Maya—but I am not quite sure how that will manifest here in my new home on the ancient Mayan soil. Moving here has not been unlike walking into a cave as part of some rite of passage—with more to come.

In the meanwhile, we discuss the reverent relocation and removal of the bats with Darrin. He assures us that he and his crew know how to do this in a safe way.

Now to the matter of the bees.

Bee: "Sweet results await if you are willing to get your ego out of the way and immerse yourself in the connected energy of all things. When you connect with the Great Hive you are vibrating and buzzing in exquisite harmony with all. When you "self-forget" you remember that you are part of a greater, unified consciousness." —*The Spirit Animal Oracle*, Colette Baron-Reid

July 16, 2019: Capricorn Full Moon, Lunar Eclipse

I bury some of the dead bees in my Capricorn Full Moon ceremony. Feeling sad yet reverent, I make sure they are honored on this property. I include them strategically and reverently in my Full Moon clearing—they and their sweet, tangy honey will always be a part of this space going forward.

Full Moon Intention: I honor all that was and ever will be, trusting the circle of life with reverence and patience. I honor bee medicine for bringing acute awareness to pain that needs acknowledging through its sting and healing my evolution with the sweetness of its honey.

July 17, 2019: Asking for Help

I'm a medium, so experiencing spirits isn't scary or outside of my box of tricks. However, this feels different. I told Dennis that we woke the dead and they are angry. Specifically, I was hearing from two men and a mean woman. I asked the cosmos for help in shifting and transmuting the darkness out of this property.

July 31, 2019: Leo New Moon

As fate would have it, we are introduced to a famous Mayan healer up the road in the next village over, called Maya Center. Her husband, Mr. Ernesto, greets me at the door of their cottage which is a couple of miles from the entrance to

Cocksomb Basin Wildlife Sanctuary. Their place includes a shop and Mayan teaching center—and it's also a sacred site, Nu'uk Che'il. Mr. Ernesto welcomes me into the shop where I see a virtual mecca of tinctures, herbs and Mayan replicated tools, pottery and handmade textiles, and jewelry. An altar is set up in the corner with all sorts of flowers, rich incense, treats and sacred trinkets. He listens kindly as I explain that I don't have a sore throat or upset stomach, but I'm here for something else. He says, "Oh, I see. She will know what to do."

Mrs. Aurora walks in. Petite, beautiful smooth skin, smocked dress, looking to be in her early 60's. She is small in stature but her presence is gigantic. I feel like I'm meeting a celebrity.

She has me sit across from her in a hot room with a ceiling fan and fluorescent light. She hands me a crystal ball about the size of a tennis ball and has me swirl it in my right palm, moving my hand gently in a circular motion, while she quietly gazes into it. She stares at me for a few minutes, contemplative.

She says she sees a cloud in my auric field, and that I'm being spiritually attacked. For the first time in all my magical, mystical, witchy encounters, I'm out of my league. I thank her and ask her what to do.

Aurora scribbles out a prescription of herbs, assignments, and appointments on a piece of paper. She tells me Dennis will have to come, too, that she needs to see us both, because we are both being affected and it will take both of us to clear it.

August 1, 2019: Clearing Ceremony

The clearing ceremony begins. Mrs. Aurora had instructed me to begin our clearing on August 1st. August is an important month for change in the Mayan culture and calendar. Limes, eggs, smoke, copal, salt around the house, herbal baths and herbal cleaning solutions. We aren't allowed to do ceremony on Mondays, Wednesdays, or Saturdays, as those are the sacred days of the spirits buried on our property—and when, as Mrs. Aurora has told us, the spirits have power over the Earth. So, Tuesdays, Thursdays, Fridays and Sundays we are following her instructions to a "T". You'd think a husband would not be into this, but Dennis is willing to consider our options. He also senses the heaviness on the land since the tree removal.

So, I've been living in a Mayan ceremony while writing this book. In fact, my ceremony is ongoing. In fact, my whole life is ceremony.

Leo New Moon and Ceremony Intention: We embrace the wisdom of the land, the lives that have come before us and will walk in front of us with courage, honesty, and integrity. In the darkness of the Leo New Moon and the fresh energies of a new month, we ask for a clearing and cleansing of any lower vibrational energies. May those darker energies be transmuted into pure, positive potential from this day forward. And so it is.

August 7, 2019: Validation

It's been confirmed: we indeed woke the dead when we removed the trees. Darrin grins when he reports there are at least three bodies buried on our property. My husband tells Darrin, "Yup, and Amanda can tell you where to find all three of them!" Darrin - freaked out and in amazement - laughs and says, "Whoa!"

Onward, into the great unknown...

Aries full Moon

WHEN THE FULL MOON IS IN ARIES

When the Full Moon falls in the Fire sign of Aries, you can expect some sparks to fly. You might notice extra energy, including some sassy and spirited vibes. This is the perfect Moon to close the door on self-prohibiting behaviors, self-sacrifice, and any blocks you have subconsciously created. This is the Moon of the pioneer and the spiritual warrior. It's time to bang the drum of self-confidence and look at the world with fresh eyes.

Aries is the first sign in the zodiac and is represented by the Ram. It is a Fire sign, ruled by the planet Mars.

Positive (High) Vibes of the Aries Full Moon

(*Set intentions for closure or completion in these areas*)
Hobbies, habits, and health routines that no longer serve you
Drive that has resulted in overcommitment
High energy that has resulted in overstimulation
Pioneering spirit that has exhausted you
Anything that has blocked new beginnings
Anything that prevents mental wellness
Anything that takes away from your personal responsibility
Any blocks to your assertiveness, confidence, and individuality
Any blocks to authentic and genuine communication
Any selfish, self-centered, self-righteous, self-delusional, or self-seeking behaviors that have become unhealthy for you

Challenging (Low) Vibes of the Aries Full Moon

(*What you might intend to remove*)

Know-it-all attitudes
Bossy-ness
Short temper
Defensiveness
Dealing with enemies

Antagonistic attitudes
Conflicts
Self-centered viewpoint

In Health, Aries Governs

(Areas of the body where you might wish for healing)

Head
Spinal cord
Face
Brain
Complexion
Solar Plexus Chakra (Manipura Chakra)

Sample Wishes for the Full Moon in Aries

- • - I easily find myself stopping unhealthy eating habits.
- • - I'm comfortable standing up for myself, not against the other person.
- • - I embrace a total healing in the area of my head and face.

Aries Full Moon Intention

My head and heart interconnect synchronistically, allowing me to feel peace and serenity from the inside out. I find peace in the process.

Aries Full Moon Healing Invocation

I connect with my potential through patience and awareness.

Word to the Wise

When the Moon is Aries, you are likely feeling hot, possibly irritable, and ready for action. Depending on your personal constituency and situation, you may enjoy the Fire energy. But if things are feeling too heated, you can incorporate elements from the opposite sign throughout the day to balance things out. The opposite sign of Aries is the Air sign Libra. Consider contemplative activities such as a walking meditation in a labyrinth to combine action (Fire) with mindfulness (Air). Combining Air and Fire elements assists you in transmuting your intentions into the highest and brightest frequencies.

Working with Corresponding Elements

We suggest using one or more items of your choice from each element when designing your ceremony. Use as many or as few as you like.

ARIES **Fire** items: Candles + Smoke

- Red and pink candles - love
- Spicy scented candles, herbal bundles, or incense:
    - Frankincense - holiness
    - Clove - purification
    - Cinnamon - abundance

ARIES **Earth** items: Crystals + Stones

- Bloodstone - protection
- Shungite - groundedness
- Agate - balancing
- Red Jasper - spiritual grounding

ARIES **Air** items: Intentions + Mantras

- Any personal wishes you want to make in the areas Aries governs + the High Vibe Aspects of Aries
- Aries Full Moon Intention
- Aries Full Moon Healing Invocation

ARIES **Water** items: Essential Oils + Flower Essences

- Myrrh - restorative
- Cedar - cleansing
- Spruce - grounding
- Ylang Ylang - harmonizing
- Geranium - uplifting

ARIES FULL MOON NUMEROLOGY

There are many ways to incorporate numerology when formulating your ceremony. You can find numbers to work with in the degree of the sign, the date, the hour you conduct the ceremony, etc. The Full Moon Numerology Empowerment Code is a special formula developed by Amanda Rieger Green, MPH at Wise Skies. We like to think of this as part of our secret sauce. We use this number to find synchronicities as well as journaling on the day of the New Moon.

Aries Full Moon Numerology Empowerment Code = 8

Numbers have power. We add the numbers that correlate with the Sun sign and the Moon sign, to create a unique code to use in ceremonies. During the Full Moon, the Sun and the Moon appear in opposite zodiac signs. That means each one is assigned a number according to the Moon's zodiac sign and it's opposite.

The Wise Skies Formula:
Aries Numerology = 1
Libra Numerology = 7
Sun in Aries (1) + Moon in Libra (7) = 8

The "8" Empowerment Code promotes focus on balancing internal and external value as well as gratitude. Notice when you see an 8 today: it's a reminder to stay open-minded to opportunities of abundance both inside and out. The 8 will encourage you to trust your internal value-system to manifest a rich experience externally. Seeing an 8 reminds you to pause and thank your lucky stars. When you show gratitude, you will know gratitude. It can enhance your ceremony to incorporate 8 of anything in your design.

Numerology Code Journaling

- *When do I feel worthy or valuable? How does that reflect abundance in my experiences?*
- *Am I willing to let go of any specific fears in the energy of the Aries Full Moon in order to experience more abundance both internally (in my mind) and externally (in my world)?*

ARIES FULL MOON CEREMONY
Free to Be Me

This ceremony guides you in removing anything that suppresses your unique spirit. With a combination of crystals, essential oils, energy healing, visualization, and alchemy, this an ideal ceremony for anyone who is feeling stuck. Use the Aries Full Moon ceremony to put an end to egotistical thinking, and anything that holds you back from moving forward with your life.

BEFORE YOU BEGIN GATHERING TOOLS, SAY THE FULL MOON INVOCATION FOUND ON PAGE XX.

Step One: Selecting Tools

Set up a Full Moon wishing area in a quiet space without distractions. Ideally you can do this outdoors, but a private space inside works too. Refer to the corresponding elements in the section above to select your tools. We suggest incorporating at least one tool per element (Fire, Earth, Air, Water), as well as a journal to write your intentions and responses to the journal prompts. You'll also need a few cinnamon sticks and a calming, decaffeinated tea (we like chamomile, raspberry leaf, or holy basil).

Step Two: Purge

Before the Aries Full Moon is exact, write about any negative feelings, thoughts, and behaviors that have been surfacing for you since the previous New Moon (over the past two weeks). Consider any frustrations, limitations, and irritants.

Step Three: Oils & Crystals

Pour 8 (Aries Full Moon Empowerment Code) drops of essential oil(s) on your right hand, then dab the oil along the lumbar spine, specifically the three lower chakra areas from the sacrum through the lumbar spinal column (Root, Sacral & Solar Plexus). Adjust your pelvis, sitting up straight and aligning the spinal column. Inhale and exhale deeply three times. Place the crystals you want to work with in your right hand (the right side of the body expels energy) with a couple of drops of essential oils. Deeply inhale and exhale a few times to clear your energy.

Step Four: Clearing Meditation

Light a candle, or start a Fire in a pit or Fireplace if that is an option. Gaze into the flames. Carefully hold a cinnamon stick over the candle flame or drop several cinnamon sticks into the Fire pit. Breath in the Earthy aroma.

Soften your body and become receptive to any additional energies or intentions you become aware of that may need to be cleared and purged. Ask your body—specifically the Root (security), Sacral (emotions), and Solar Plexus (ego) chakras—to clear, recalibrate, and balance in order to unblock any energetic stagnation or disease, and to address what needs to be healed in order to move forward.

Step Five: Intentions

With this new clarity and energetic reset, use your list of challenges and anything that came to mind during meditation to write your Full Moon intentions at the time the Full Moon is exact (or within a few hours). Write out the below invocation on the back side of your paper:

I am willing to dismiss the following limiting behaviors/beliefs once and for all.

[LIST BEHAVIORS/BELIEFS]

I am allowing my body to naturally process lower vibrational emotions such as_____ with grace and ease.

I request the illumination of the Aries Full Moon and my own Energy Chakras to shed light on my shadows with the intention of being in alignment with my Highest Self and for the Greatest Good.

Write any personalized wishes or intentions you wish to include in the ceremony.

Step Six: Alchemy

Go outside under the light of the Moon with your crystals and light a small candle (or light your Fire pit). Bless and liberate your intentions by carefully burning the paper in the flame of the candle. Ask the Aries Full Moon to raise your frequency by transmuting anything of lower vibration into a higher vibration. In this way, you are incorporating the alchemy of the cosmos to shift what is dense and dark into pure, positive potential light. Ask the Universe to shift all challenges into abundance in the flame of Divine light. Leave the crystals out for three nights under the Aries Full Moon. If you cannot leave them outside, place them in a window sill.

Step Seven: Tea & Magic

Now that you have set your intentions into motion, go inside and brew yourself a calming tea. Find a quiet spot to get centered and drink your tea. Relax and trust in the unfolding of your own growth and healing.

After three days, retrieve your crystals with a thankful heart. Keep the crystals in your pocket, next to your bed, in your car, or somewhere close over the next two weeks. Continue communication with them, acknowledging and thanking them often for their support and intelligence.

Step Eight: Closing Sacred Space

It is important to seal the energy after any ceremony. Refer to **page xx** for our suggestion on closing sacred space, or say your personalized closing prayers.

MAKING IT PERSONAL

Moon Musings
- Amanda

The Full Moon in Aries always happens when the Sun is in Libra, my Sun sign. This Moon serves as my personal check-point in my birthday month and an opportunity to let go of anything that limits my individuality, motivation, and voice. Being a Libra, I sometimes fall into lower vibes of indecisiveness, people-pleasing or procrastination. This is the Full Moon that gives my solar year the added oomph to move forward with greater clarity, integrity, and peace. Here are a few intentions from previous Aries Full Moons:

- I let go of people-pleasing behaviors, indecisiveness, and procrastination with grace and ease.
- I honor all experiences in the past year, trusting the process of my personal and spiritual evolution as divinely timed.
- Anything that limits my individual voice and soul's expression will organically shift into unlimited potential.

- I am open to constructive feedback and organically incorporate it into all aspects of my being in order to evolve spiritually in this lifetime and beyond.
- May the momentum of this fiery Full Moon help the inhabitants of this planet to become higher, brighter individuals and good stewards for their souls' purpose and the greater good.

Best Wishes

- Tiffany

The Full Moon in Aries hits in my 4th or 5th house depending on the degree of the Full Moon. So, sometimes I add elements relating to home and family (4th house) or love-given (5th house) issues. Here are a few wishes I have used on previous Aries Full Moons:

- I am willing to look at and let go of self-limiting beliefs.
- I no longer attract people who are bossy and selfish.
- I'm willing to stop doing things that drain my life force energy.
- Above all, I'm willing and ready to set aside what I think I know, and what I think I Above all, help me set aside what I think I know, and what I think I want, so that the Divine can flow through me. May I be of service to God and my fellows.

taurus full Moon

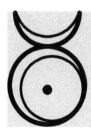

WHEN THE FULL MOON IS IN TAURUS

When the Full Moon falls in the Earth sign of Taurus, you can expect to feel centered, affectionate, and persistent. You might also notice yourself or others becoming more obstinate and sedentary. This is the perfect Moon to set intentions around removing stubborn tendencies, finding a sense of completion with work projects, and removing blocks to financial security. This is the Moon of promises, creature comforts, worthiness, and values. It's time to bang the drum of self-worth and offer a renewed sense of commitment to finalizing some area of your life.

Taurus is the second sign in the zodiac and is represented by the Bull. It is an Earth sign, ruled by the planet Venus.

Positive (High) Vibes of the Taurus Full Moon

(*Set intentions for closure or completion in these areas*)

Removing inconsistency and impatience
Forgiveness where there has been a failure or disloyalty
Stopping nurturing through unhealthy food
Negating self-worth or beating yourself up
Awareness of which core values and manners need to shift
Removing blocks to financial security
Letting go of any unhealthy sensuality and pleasure
Finding security and stability through slow and steady growth
Finding contentment through perseverance

Challenging (Low) Vibes of the Taurus Full Moon

(*What you might intend to remove*)

Stubbornness
Laziness
Slow to change or make decisions
Tire-kicking

Overly protective or territorial
Possessiveness
Attachment
Stagnation

In Health, Taurus Governs

(Areas of the body where you might wish for healing)

Throat and neck
Coughs
Speech and vocal cords
Thyroid
Throat Chakra (Vishudha Chakra)
Root Chakra (Muladhara Chakra)

Sample Wishes for the Full Moon in Taurus

- I become aware of when I'm feeling lazy and replace laziness with right action.
- I request all stubborn tendencies to be removed from me.
- I put an end to financial insecurities, choosing to trust the Universe has my back.
- I no longer crave sweets in an unhealthy way.

Taurus Full Moon Intention

Fear, insecurity, and control organically process through and out of my body, creating space for more love, compassion, and trust.

Taurus Full Moon Healing Invocation

I practice consistency and open-mindedness.

Word to the Wise

When the Moon is in Taurus, you are likely feeling connected and grounded. Depending on your personal constituency and situation, you may enjoy the security and stability the Earth energy provides. But if things are feeling dense, fixed, or even stuck, you can incorporate elements from the opposite sign throughout the day to balance things out. The opposite sign of Taurus is the Water sign Scorpio. Consider Water-related activities to encourage fluidity: taking baths, drinking tea, making spritzes, using herbal sprays and tinctures, or swimming in hot springs or a lake. It can be useful to combine the steadfastness of your intentions (Earth) with the flexibility of trusting providence to flow in at divine right timing (Water).

Working with Corresponding Elements

We suggest using one or more items of your choice from each element when designing your ceremony. Use as many or as few as you like.

TAURUS **Fire** items: Candles + Smoke

- Green and brown or tan candles - nurturing
- Woodsy scents and incense:
    - Sage - clearing energy
    - Cedar - mental clarity
    - Rosemary - remembrance

TAURUS **Earth** items: Crystals + Stones

- Tiger's Eye - empowerment
- Jasper - security
- Rutilated Quartz - spiritual development
- Sodalite - authentic communication

TAURUS **Air** items: Intentions + Mantras

- Any personal wishes you want to make in the areas Taurus governs + the High Vibe Aspects of Taurus
- Taurus Full Moon Intention
- Taurus Full Moon Healing Invocation

TAURUS **Water** items: Essential Oils + Flower Essences

- Vetiver - spiritual grounding
- Rose - love
- Bergamot - letting go of fear

TAURUS FULL MOON NUMEROLOGY

There are many ways to incorporate numerology when formulating your ceremony. You can find numbers to work with in the degree of the sign, the date, the hour you conduct the ceremony, etc. The Full Moon Numerology Empowerment Code is a special formula developed by Amanda Rieger Green,

MPH at Wise Skies. We like to think of this as part of our secret sauce. We use this number to find synchronicities as well as journaling on the day of the New Moon.

Taurus Full Moon Numerology Empowerment Code = 1

Numbers have power. We add the numbers that correlate with the Sun sign and the Moon sign to create a unique code to use in ceremonies. During the Full Moon, the Sun and the Moon appear in opposite zodiac signs. That means each one is assigned a number according to the Moon's zodiac sign and it's opposite.

The Wise Skies Formula:
Taurus Numerology = 2
Scorpio Numerology = 8
Sun in Scorpio (8) + Moon in Taurus (2) = 10
Reduce it down to a single digit: 1+0 = 1

The "1" Empowerment Code promotes wholeness, stamina, and drive. Notice when you see a 1 today: it's a reminder to put yourself first. Seeing a 1 reminds you to pause and put on your own oxygen mask before helping others. It can enhance your ceremony to incorporate 1 of anything in your design.

Numerology Code Journaling

- *What are my top goals? What is limiting me from achieving those goals?*
- *Am I willing to be the leader of my life and, in the energy of the Taurus Full Moon, let go of anything holding me back from experiencing wholeness?*

TAURUS FULL MOON CEREMONY
Shapeshifting

This ceremony helps clear stubborn attitudes, behaviors and beliefs that weigh down the physical and auric fields via the process of freezing and melting Water. Using crystals, herbs, and a sacred bath, we shift energetic blocks into pure potential. This is an ideal ceremony for processing grief, or detoxifying the body, mind, or spirit.

BEFORE YOU BEGIN GATHERING TOOLS, SAY THE FULL MOON INVOCATION FOUND ON PAGE XX.

Step One: Selecting Tools

Set up a Full Moon wishing area in a quiet space without distractions. Ideally you can do this outdoors, but a private space inside works too. Refer to the corresponding elements in the section above to select your tools. We suggest incorporating at least one tool per element (Fire, Earth, Air, Water), as well as a journal to write your intentions and responses to the journal prompts. You'll also need an ice tray and some dried herbs (we like sage, rosemary, and thyme).

Step Two: Fire

Carefully ignite a bundle of sage (or dried herbs of your choice) in your kitchen over the sink. Cleanse and clear the area in your kitchen space by blowing on the sage to create smoke. Wave the sage smoke throughout the kitchen space and over your body, head to toe.

Say: *I am cleansing and clearing my energy. This space is whole, light, and filled with inspiration.*

Light a green or brown candle.

Step Three: Water

Gather the crystals you want to use, an ice tray, assorted herbs and essential oils. Fill the ice tray with Water. Put a couple of drops of essential oils in your palms, rub them together, and bring them up to your nose to inhale deeply with your eyes closed. As you exhale, begin feeling a sense of stability and centering in your body. Repeat your breath cycle two more times. Once finished, hold your hands over the Water in the ice tray.

Say: *I activate this Water with light, love, and divine conductivity.*

Put 1 (Taurus Full Moon Numerology Empowerment Code) drop of oil into the Water in each ice cube space.

Step Four: Journal

Turn on some soft or meditative music. Use the numerology journal prompts and the high, low, and health vibes of Taurus to guide your writing.

Consider anything that is limiting your light. What is blocking your ability to change, evolve, and shift into something better? Ponder any blocks you are experiencing in your energy field, and clarify what you are willing to remove in your life.

The hour the Full Moon is exact is an optimal time to write wishes, intentions, or mantras. Leave the wishes in your journal and review them throughout the coming months.

Next, write six words that describe the 'bad' behaviors that you are ready to transform. Next, write six 'good' behavior words that describe new thoughts or actions you want to replace those 'bad' behaviors. For example: "Judgmental" is a bad behavior word, while "Forgiving" is it's opposite. Be kind to yourself as you're exploring the spectrum of opposites. We are on a fact-finding mission to evolve and grow.

Once you feel settled, write those twelve words on tiny individual pieces of paper, fold them up, and drop each word into a section in the ice tray.

Step Five: Making it So

Place a few crystals into the Water in the ice tray. If you don't have enough to fill all of the slots, it's not a big deal—just intuitively spread them around. Next, sprinkle some dried herbs in the Water in the ice tray. Once you are finished, bless the tray.

Say: *I activate and bless these intentions in the Water. What is moving will become solid. And so it is.*

Place the ice tray full of goodies in the freezer.

Step Six: Soak it in

After three days, prepare a hot bath (or shower, catching a few inches of the Water in the tub with the drain closed). Relight one of your candles and set it on a bathroom counter nearby. Remove the tray of ice cubes from the freezer. After relaxing for a few minutes in the tub (or shower), drop each ice cube into the tub, one by one.

Say: *I am transmuting these energies into divine light and intelligence.*

Soak in the bath or shower, breathing in the aromas and ask for clarity. Stay in the bath or shower while it drains completely. Once there is no more Water, the ceremony is complete and you can clean up the crystals and wish papers. You can put the wish papers in your compost, a flower pot, or bury them in the ground. You can also release them outside in an area that would not be littering. However you dispose of them, we do not advise throwing the wishes in the trash.

Step Seven: Closing Sacred Space

It is important to seal the energy after any ceremony. Refer to **page xx** for our suggestion on closing sacred space, or say your personalized closing prayers.

MAKING IT PERSONAL

Moon Musings

- Amanda

The Full Moon in Taurus is an energy where I work on emotional and karmic healing because of something called an "interception" I have in my natal astrology with my Scorpio - Taurus line and because my natal Chiron (the wounded healer) is in Taurus. I consciously embrace this energy to illuminate self-limiting behaviors, stubbornness and beliefs of lack or unworthiness. It is also a Moon for financial amends (where applicable). Here are a few intentions from previous Taurus Full Moons:

- I consciously and willingly let go of stubborn attitudes and deeply rooted beliefs of unworthiness, lack, and fears that limit my abundance, self-worth, and capacity to love.

- Healing happens beautifully and naturally in my mind, body, emotions, and spirit through the illumination of the Taurus Full Moonlight.
- I am abundance consciousness.
- I honestly and compassionately share my experiences of self-doubt, mistrust, dishonesty, insecurity and shame with myself, my spirit and others. My genuine voice heals.
- Respect, honor and reverence for the Earth and all its beings happens with abundance throughout humanity. We are open vessels of love.

Best Wishes

- Tiffany

The Full Moon in Taurus hits in my 5th or 6th house depending on the degree of the Full Moon. So, sometimes I add elements relating to love-given (5th house) or health issues (6th house). Here are a few wishes I have used on previous Taurus Full Moons:

- I no longer crave sugar.
- Completion makes me feel grounded.
- I enjoy finishing what I start.
- I enjoy eating practical, simple meals that honor the Earth and all who live here.
- Endings mean beginnings.
- All is well in my kingdom.
- Above all, help me set aside what I think I know, and what I think I want, so that the Divine can flow through me. May I be of service to God and my fellows.

Gemini full Moon

WHEN THE FULL MOON IS IN GEMINI

When the Full Moon falls in the Air sign of Gemini, you can expect plans to change. You might notice a need to be around friends, be social, and to keep a lot of tabs open on your computer. This is the perfect Moon to find closure by talking it out, sending a final newsletter, or finishing a book. This is the Moon of the multi-tasker, the social butterfly, and the curious Seeker. It is time to bang the drum of self-inquisition and approach the world with a fresh perspective: we're all crewmates on the same boat.

Gemini is the third sign in the zodiac and is represented by the Twins. It is an Air sign, ruled by the planet Mercury.

Positive (High) Vibes of the Gemini Full Moon

(*Set intentions for closure or completion in these areas*)

No more multi-tasking that dilutes your ability to complete tasks
Hyper-focus and attention to detail that causes analysis paralysis
Any blocks to writing, editing, speaking, and reading
Any blocks to clear communication and healthy discussions
Anything blocking you from mental health and well-being
Any setbacks to micro goals
Ending social opportunities that have drained you

Challenging (Low) Vibes of the Gemini Full Moon

(*What you might intend to remove*)

Overcommitment
Overthinking
Detachment
Indecision
Impulsivity
Anxieties

In Health, Gemini Governs

Lungs and breathing
Shoulders and collar bone
Arms, wrists, and hands
Nervous system
Throat Chakra (Vishuddha Chakra)
Third Eye (Anja Chakra)

Sample Wishes for the Full Moon in Gemini

- I am willing to stop creating chaos, confusion, and any crazy-making behaviors.
- I can easily finish writing a book that brings good information to the world.
- I find the best team of medical professionals help me heal my lungs, wrists, and nervous system.

Gemini Full Moon Intention

I detach from fear, mistrust and secrecy in all communications and actions. The right and left hemispheres of my brain synchronize, facilitating mental clarity, empowered discernment and innate trust in every experience as part of the process.

Gemini Full Moon Healing Invocation

I effectively synthesize all experiences and practice focus.

Word to the Wise

When the Moon is in Gemini, it's possible you are feeling pulled in many directions. Depending on your personal constituency and situation, you may enjoy the endless options provided under an Air-Moon. But if things are feeling too indecisive and scattered, you can incorporate elements from the opposite sign throughout the day to balance things out. The opposite sign of Gemini is Sagittarius. Consider contemplative yoga or something that combines thought (Air) with action (Fire).

Working with Corresponding Elements

We suggest using one or more items of your choice from each element when designing your ceremony. Use as many or as few as you like.

GEMINI **Fire** items: Candles + Smoke

- Blue and yellow candles - stimulating
- Uplifting citrus and herbal scented candles, herbal bundles, or incense:
    - Lavender - calming
    - Sage - clearing
    - Orange - uplifting

GEMINI **Earth** items: Crystals + Stones

- Labradorite - magic
- Aquamarine - letting go
- Blue or Green Kyanite - alignment
- Rainbow Obsidian - auric grounding
- Apache Tear - energetic clarity

GEMINI **Air** items: Intentions + Mantras

- Any personal wishes you want to make in the areas Gemini governs + the High Vibe Aspects of Gemini
- Gemini Full Moon Intention
- Gemini Full Moon Healing Invocation

GEMINI **Water** items: Essential Oils + Flower Essences

- Basil - blessings
- Neroli - sensual comfort
- Orange - cheerful
- Lemon - zest
- Citrus - uplifting
- Grapefruit - spiritual clearing

GEMINI FULL MOON NUMEROLOGY

There are many ways to incorporate numerology when formulating your ceremony. You can find numbers to work with in the degree of the sign, the date, the hour you conduct the ceremony, etc. The Full Moon Numerology Empowerment Code is a special formula developed by Amanda Rieger Green, MPH at Wise Skies. We like to think of this as part of our secret sauce. We

use this number to find synchronicities as well as journaling on the day of the New Moon.

Gemini Full Moon Numerology Empowerment Code = 3

Numbers have power. We add the numbers that correlate with the Sun sign and the Moon sign, to create a unique code to use in ceremonies. During the Full Moon, the Sun and the Moon appear in opposite zodiac signs. That means each one is assigned a number according to the Moon's zodiac sign and it's opposite.

The Wise Skies Formula:
Gemini Numerology = 3
Sagittarius Numerology = 9
Sun in Sagittarius (9) + Moon in Gemini (3) = 12
Reduce it down to a single digit: 1+2 = 3

The "3" Empowerment Code promotes communication, clarity, and creativity. Notice when you see a 3 today: it's a reminder to get creative and express yourself. The 3 energy will promote clear, conscious communication and the ability to socialize with ease. Seeing a 3 reminds you to pause and get curious. It can enhance your ceremony to incorporate 3 of anything in your design.

Numerology Code Journaling

- *Where do I take on too many projects at once and lack follow-through, efficiency and completion?*
- *Am I willing to stop spreading myself too thin in the energy of the Gemini Full Moon in order to experience more flow and abundance?*

GEMINI FULL MOON CEREMONY
Clarity Infusion

This ceremony offers an opportunity to discern where you can bury the hatchet and move forward in peace. Go for it! This is about your freedom. This is an ideal ceremony for anyone looking for clarity or seeking to quiet the mind. It is also a great ceremony for couples who are wanting to come to a resolution or find mutual solutions.

BEFORE YOU BEGIN GATHERING TOOLS, SAY THE FULL MOON INVOCATION FOUND ON PAGE XX.

Step One: Selecting Tools

Set up a Full Moon wishing area in a quiet space without distractions. Ideally you can do this outdoors, but a private space inside works too. Refer to the corresponding elements in the section above to select your tools. We suggest incorporating at least one tool per element (Fire, Earth, Air, Water), as well as a journal to write your intentions and responses to the journal prompts. You'll also need a clear glass or glass pitcher.

Step Two: Fill Your Cup

Fill a pitcher or glass with Water. Add any of the recommended Gemini Full Moon crystals to the Water along with 3 (Gemini Full Moon Numerology Empowerment Code) drops of the suggested essential oil you want to work with.

Say: *I am infusing and charging this Water with intellectual clarity, purity of heart and quantum energy. Repeat 3 times.*

Step Three: Willingness in Action

Write out these questions and answer them in your journal:

- *Is there any anger, resentment, or unrest I'm hanging on to?*
- *Am I willing to stop fighting anything that traps me in a state of resistance?*
- *Why or why not?*
- *Am I willing to objectively view my contribution to any of the resistance or challenges I am facing?*

- *Where can I bury the hatchet, forgive myself and others, and move forward in peace?*

Meditate on your responses. Use your breath to inhale each question and exhale each response. Take your time to tap into the energy of each response, especially where you are uncomfortable or resistant.

Make a list of all behaviors, thoughts, and actions you are willing to stop.

Step Four: Intentions

With this new clarity, write your Full Moon intentions at the time the Full Moon is exact (or within a few hours if possible). Check out our sample wishes in the section above for some wishing ideas.

Step Five: Charge the Water

Under the light of the Full Moon, place the pitcher or glass of Water on top of the peice of paper with what you are wanting to remove. Let's call it your "let-go" list. Ignite a bundle of dried lavender and wave the smoke around the glass or pitcher, your let-go list, and all around yourself.

Say: *I invoke the illumination and wisdom of the Gemini Full Moon to activate and purify in the highest light.* Repeat 3 times.

*If you cannot place the glass or pitcher outside, placing it on or near a window seat or patio.

Leave the Water and let-go list outside under the moonlight for two nights.

Step Six: Let it Go

On the third day or evening take the infused, super-charged Water inside for a bathing ceremony. Light a blue or yellow candle and place it safely on a bathroom counter nearby. Turn on some soft clearing music, such as Tibetan singing bowls, or a chakra clearing meditation.

Draw a bath and add the charged Water to it. Stir the bath Water with your hand 3 times counterclockwise. Add in a few drops of essential oils that won't burn your skin. If no bath is possible, you can sprinkle or spritz the Water over yourself in a shower.

Step Seven: Wash it Away

Read your let-go list aloud in the bath and intend that the Water will cleanse and clear your energy field from anything limiting you. Give yourself permission to find the willingness, open-mindedness, strength, and integrity to surrender anything and anyone that is diminishing your light.

After you get out of the bath or shower, light the dried lavender bundle again. Smudge the Water by waving the smoke from the lavender bundle all around the top of the Water in your bath, or the droplets from your shower. Drain the bath, then smudge yourself from head to toe.

Say: *I am anointed with discernment and enhanced vision. I am at peace.*

Blow any remaining darkness or stubbornness into the light of the candle, extinguishing the flame. Put a few drops of essential oils behind your ears and on the back of your neck daily for the next two weeks while the Moon is waning. The scents act as a comforting reminder to your cells that you are done with everything on your let-go list and ready to stand in your own strength and light.

Step Eight: Closing Sacred Space

It is important to seal the energy after any ceremony. Refer to **page xx** for our suggestion on closing sacred space, or say your personalized closing prayers.

MAKING IT PERSONAL

Moon Musings

- *Amanda*

The Gemini Full Moon is usually an insightful and powerfully illuminating Moon for me because Gemini is on the cusp of my 12th house. I usually journal on the insights, aggravations, triggers and fears that arise the couple of weeks before the Full Moon and use those as clues for letting go of negative aspects and detoxing my psyche (12th house). No small thing, right? Here are a few intentions from previous Gemini Full Moons:

- I recognize and process shame, self-critical attitudes, and judgmental thoughts with ease and self-compassion.

- My unconscious self and conscious self intercommunicate with clarity and precision for my highest good in this lifetime and throughout all lines of time.
- My conscious and unconscious healing reconciles stubborn karma. I am a channel of the highest light for the greatest good.
- Intelligence comes onto the planet with love and light.

Best Wishes

- Tiffany

The Full Moon in Gemini hits in my 6th or 7th house depending on the degree of the Moon. So, sometimes I add elements relating to health (6th house) or relationships (7th house).

- I enjoy participating in a book club and easily read all of the material on time.
- I'm willing to stop doing things that create confusion.
- Above all, help me set aside what I think I know, and what I think I want, so that the Divine can flow through me. May I be of service to God and my fellows.

Cancer full Moon

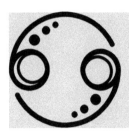

WHEN THE FULL MOON IS IN CANCER

When the Full Moon falls in the Water sign of Cancer, you can expect emotional intelligence to reign supreme. Cancer is the Moon's home sign, and Luna is quite comfortable here. You may feel like nesting and finding comfort in home-cooked meals: keep the home Fires burning. If you notice controlling behaviors and obsessive-compulsive patterns, that's part of the bad behaviors of this Moon sign - consider where you can let someone off the hook. This is the perfect Moon to complete a home improvement project, conduct a house blessing, or clear your personal blocks. This is the Moon of the Mother archetype as well as the Intuitive Counselor. There is a yearning to nurture and be nurtured. It's time to bang the drum of self-care and healthy relationships. *Hey! You may dig our House or Business Blessing - it's free at www. WiseSkiesAdvice.com.*

Cancer is the fourth sign of the zodiac and is represented by the Crab. It is a Water sign, ruled by the Moon.

Positive (High) Vibes of the Cancer Full Moon

(Set intentions for closure or completion in these areas)

Any closure needed around home, mothering, and family
A sense of completion with overly nurturing and offering excessive caregiving
Anything blocking your kindness and compassion
Anything getting in the way of emotional intelligence and intuition
Anything blocking your empathy and sensitivity to others
Healing early childhood conditioning and self-compassion

Challenging (Low) Vibes of the Cancer Full Moon

(What you might intend to remove)

Being controlling
Perfectionism
Being over-protective

Insecurity
Obsessiveness
Fear of rejection
Lack of clear ambitions
Being moody or crabby

In Health, Cancer Governs

Chest
Breast
Ribs
Stomach
Pancreas
Tumors
Digestive system
Third Eye (Anja)
Heart Chakra (Anahata)

Sample Wishes for the Full Moon in Cancer

- All is well in my kingdom.
- Home is where the heart is.
- I experience a complete and total healing in my heart and chest.

Cancer Full Moon Intention

I recognize fears, insecurities, and intimidation as limitations that hold me back, and am willing to dismiss any darkness that impedes my light. I feel empowered to open up and shine.

Cancer New Moon Healing Invocation

I experience my emotions in the present moment and know it is safe to process them naturally.

Word to the Wise

When the Moon is in Cancer, it's possible you are feeling heightened emotions, increased intuition, and more empathetic. Depending on your personal constituency and situation, you may enjoy the emotional depth provided under a Water-Moon. But if things are feeling too heavy, you can incorporate elements from the opposite sign throughout the day to balance things out. The opposite sign of Cancer is Capricorn. Consider drumming, walking on the ground outside with bare feet, or visualizing roots growing through your feet to the center of the Earth in meditation to combine emotions (Water) with stability and practical outcomes (Earth). Combining Water and Earth elements assists you in anchoring your intentions with practical action.

Working with Corresponding Elements

We suggest using one or more items of your choice from each element when designing your ceremony. Use as many or as few as you like.

CANCER **Fire** items: Candles + Smoke

- Candle (white or off-white) - purification
- Neutral scented candles, herbal bundles, or incense:
    - Camomile - calm
    - Jasmine - upliftment
    - Peppermint - emotional processing

CANCER **Earth** items: Crystals + Stones

- Rose Quartz - unconditional love
- Moonstone - intuition
- Pink or Watermelon Tourmaline - emotional stability

CANCER **Air** items: Intentions + Mantras

- Any personal wishes you want to make in the areas Cancer governs + the High Vibe Aspects of Cancer
- Cancer Full Moon Intention
- Cancer Full Moon Healing Invocation

CANCER **Water** items: Essential Oils + Flower Essences

- Rosemary - passion
- Fennel - nurturing
- Juniper - emotional processing

CANCER FULL MOON NUMEROLOGY

There are many ways to incorporate numerology when formulating your ceremony. You can find numbers to work with in the degree of the sign, the date, the hour you conduct the ceremony, etc. The Full Moon Numerology Empowerment Code is a special formula developed by Amanda Rieger Green,

MPH at Wise Skies. We like to think of this as part of our secret sauce. We use this number to find synchronicities as well as journaling on the day of the New Moon.

Cancer Full Moon Numerology Empowerment Code = 5

Numbers have power. We add the numbers that correlate with the Sun sign and the Moon sign, to create a unique code to use in ceremonies. During the Full Moon, the Sun and the Moon appear in opposite zodiac signs. That means each one is assigned a number according to the Moon's zodiac sign and it's opposite.

The Wise Skies Formula:
Cancer Numerology = 4
Capricorn Numerology = 10
Sun in Capricorn (10) + Moon in Cancer (4) = 14
Reduce it down to a single digit: 1+4 = 5

The "5" Empowerment Code helps us see where we are inconsistent, chaotic, and restless. Sometimes we create drama when all we really want is personal freedom. Notice when you see a 5 today: it's a reminder to lose the drama and set yourself free from disruptive attitudes and behaviors. Seeing a 5 reminds you to pause and find abundance in the stillness. It can enhance your ceremony to incorporate 5 of anything in your design.

Numerology Code Journaling

- *When do I feel restless and unsettled? Am I willing to do something different to change the way I feel?*
- *In the energy of the Cancer Full Moon, where can I let go of unnecessary drama or anxiety-making behaviors in order to experience more peace, stability, and groundedness?*

CANCER FULL MOON CEREMONY
My Body is My Temple

It's important to take care of our home-body by regularly clearing our energy field. This powerful ceremony can be done more simply with epsom salt alone each time you shower.

BEFORE YOU BEGIN GATHERING TOOLS, SAY THE FULL MOON INVOCATION FOUND ON PAGE XX.

Step One: Selecting Tools

Set up a Full Moon wishing area in a quiet space without distractions. Ideally you can do this outdoors, but a private space inside works too. Refer to the corresponding elements in the section above to select your tools. We suggest incorporating at least one tool per element (Fire, Earth, Air, Water), as well as a journal to write your intentions and responses to the journal prompts. You'll also need some epsom salts and dried rose petals for this ceremony.

Step Two: Clearing Body Scrub

When the Full Moon is exact (or within a few hours), light a white or off-white candle and set it on the counter to burn while you create the scrub. Write your wishes, intentions, and invocations on small strips of paper from your journal.

Gather the salts, rose petals, wishes, intentions, and a mixing bowl. You can choose the amount you wish to make based on the amount of salt and roses you have. However, for one scrub, about two cups of salts and one large rose head will do.

Pour the salts, wishes, and rose petals into the mixing bowl with a few drops of essential oil. Mix this with your hands. Let this time mixing be a short meditation, inhaling and exhaling intentionally as you stir.

*Optional: We recommend making a big batch of the clearing body scrub and keeping it in your bath or shower area to scrub yourself each time you bathe during the following 2 weeks while the Cancer Full Moon wanes.

Step Three: Create Calm

Take the lit candle into the bathroom with you and set it on a nearby counter in a safe place. Dim the lights and turn on some soft music.

Prepare a warm shower. If you don't have a shower you can take a bath, however this is not intended to be a soak. You'll want to use this like you would a body scrub. Why? This is an optimal time to clear your energy field with Water and salt, removing and transmuting lower vibrational energies rather than soaking them in.

Say: *I am preparing space to cleanse, clear, and transmute any dark energies into pure positive light with healing Waters. And so it is.*

Step Four: Sacred Shower

Take a normal shower as usual (wash your hAir, etc.). Once you've showered, grab a handful of your scrub and begin by gently and mindfully scrubbing your head (yes, your head), face (unless this will irritate you), neck, shoulders, arms, chest, back, stomach, hips, and so on all the way to the soles of your feet while still standing in the shower with the Water running over you..

Say: *I am cleansing and clearing my energy. I am transmuting and transforming any lower vibrations in to pure positive light. Any energy that is not mine is compassionately transferred back to whom it belongs. All aspects of my Soul and Self are here now.* Repeat this three times.

Stand still. Breathe. Allow the Cancer Full Moon to clear anything holding you back and limiting your unconditional love. You are worthy. You are whole. Breathe in and know that truth in every fiber of your being. Towel off and get ready to experience the rest of the day or evening from a pure new state of being.

*Option: repeat each time you shower for the next two weeks as the Lunar cycle comes to a close.

Step Five: Closing Sacred Space

It is important to seal the energy after any ceremony. Refer to **page xx** for our suggestion on closing sacred space, or say your personalized closing prayers.

MAKING IT PERSONAL

Moon Musings
- Amanda

My ascendent is Cancer, and my natal 4th house (ruled by Cancer) is loaded with planets. Planets, thus the Cancer Full Moon is an opportunity for me to shed and emotionally process anything that limits my authentic connection to hEarth and home. It's also a Moon where I can celebrate family (both my family of origin and chosen tribe). Here are a few moon musings from previous Cancer Full Moons:

- Honoring all of my emotions with integrity and a healthy attitude feels comforting, authentic, and healthy.
- I interconnect my head and my heart with discernment and grace.
- Healthy vulnerability rather than detachment or disassociation happens in my relationships with peace and ease.
- Nurture and compassion flows to and through me.
- My insides match my outsides. I am genuine with myself and others and easily let go of inauthentic communication.
- Home is where the heart is. Trusting my heart happens naturally.
- Peace, love, and comfort pulses throughout the cosmos.

Best Wishes
- Tiffany

The Full Moon in Cancer hits in my 7th or 8th house depending on the degree of the New Moon. So sometimes I add elements relating to relationships (7th house) or shared resources (8th house). Here are a few wishes I have used on previous Cancer Full Moons:

- I no longer crave foods that are unhealthy for me: I thrive on simple and interesting vegan foods, that delight me, nourish me, and taste good.
- Home is a place I run to, not away from.
- My home is my sanctuary. I'm willing to remove all items that are not conducive to an enchanting, vibrant living space.
- I feel comfortable, radiant, and at home in my body.

- I let go of any false beliefs behind feminine relationships; I am deeply connected to the Divine Mother and Goddess energy.
- Above all, help me set aside what I think I know, and what I think I want, so that the Divine can flow through me. May I be of service to God and my fellows.

Leo full Moon

WHEN THE FULL MOON IS IN LEO

When the Full Moon falls in the Fire sign of Leo, you can expect heat to rise. Entertainment, passion, strength, neediness, attention-seeking, and stubbornness are all on the spectrum of Leo themes. This is the perfect Moon to set intentions around playfulness and having more fun with life. This is the Moon of the heart-centered leader. It's time to bang the drum of courage and look at the world through rose colored glasses. Everyone deserves more unconditional Leo-like love, not less.

Leo is the fifth sign in the zodiac and is represented by the Lion. It is a Fire sign, ruled by the Sun.

Positive (High) Vibes of the Leo Full Moon

(Set intentions for closure or completion in these areas)

Completing any leadership activities
Finding courage
Removing blocks to passion, play, and generosity
Recognizing people with appreciation
Giving yourself permission to *not* be loyal to unhealthy people or situations
Removing blocks to any vitality
Removing blocks to trusting your instincts

Challenging (Low) Vibes of the Leo Full Moon

(What you might intend to remove)

Neediness
Attention-Seeking tendencies
Self-centered behaviors
Inability to experience and truly express gratitude
Unrealistic expectations

In Health, Leo Governs

(Areas of the body where you might wish for healing)

Heart
Spinal Cord
Crown Chakra (Sahasrara Chakra)
Heart Chakra (Anahata Chakra)

Sample Wishes for the Full Moon in Leo

- I absolve any neediness and insecurities that have built up in my DNA.
- I am courageous. I am no longer afraid of being the star of my own life
- I am deeply bonded to myself, there is no room for doubt or self-consciousness in my auric field.

Leo Full Moon Intention

I tap into my pure potential and trust its unfolding. I acknowledge and surrender my ego-based fears.

Leo Full Moon Healing Invocation

I generate passion and abundance with myself and those around me with no strings attached.

Word to the Wise

When the Moon is in Leo, you are likely feeling hot, and possibly curious for attention and affection. Depending on your personal constituency and situation, you may enjoy the Fire energy. But if things are feeling too heated, you can incorporate elements from the opposite sign throughout the day to balance things out. The opposite sign of Leo is the Air sign Aquarius. Consider contemplative activities like a walking meditation in a labyrinth to combine action (Fire) with mindfulness (Air). Getting into action (Leo) for groups (Aquarius) through volunteerism is another idea to encourage equanimity.

Working with Corresponding Elements

We suggest using one or more items of your choice from each element when designing your ceremony. Use as many or as few as you like.

LEO **Fire** items: Candles + Smoke

- Red and green candles - love
- Citrus scented candles, herbal bundles, or incense:
  - Palo Santo - protection
  - Grapefruit - uplifting
  - Mandarin - enlightening
  - Lemon - brightening

LEO **Earth** items: Crystals + Stones

- Pyrite - strength
- Fuchsite - head & heart
- Sunstone - vitality

LEO **Air** items: Intentions + Mantras

- Any personal wishes you want to make in the areas Leo governs + the High Vibe Aspects of Leo
- Leo Full Moon Intention
- Leo Full Moon Healing Invocation

LEO **Water** items: Essential Oils + Flower Essences

- Myrrh - restorative
- Cedar - cleansing
- Spruce - grounding
- Ylang Ylang - harmonizing
- Geranium - uplifting

LEO FULL MOON NUMEROLOGY

There are many ways to incorporate numerology when formulating your ceremony. You can find numbers to work with in the degree of the sign, the date, the hour you conduct the ceremony, etc. The Full Moon Numerology Empowerment Code is a special formula developed by Amanda Rieger Green, MPH at Wise Skies. We like to think of this as part of our secret sauce. We use this number to find synchronicities as well as journaling on the day of the New Moon.

Full Moon Numerology Empowerment Code = 7

Numbers have power. We add the numbers that correlate with the Sun sign and the Moon sign, to create a unique code to use in ceremonies. During the Full

Moon, the Sun and the Moon appear in opposite zodiac signs. That means each one is assigned a number according to the Moon's zodiac sign and it's opposite.

The Wise Skies Formula:
Leo Numerology = 5
Aquarius Numerology = 11 Master Number
Sun in Aquarius (11) + Moon in Leo (5) = 16
Reduce it down to a single digit: 1+6 = 7

The "7" Empowerment Code offers themes around wisdom, discernment, and detachment. Notice when you see a 7 today: it's a reminder to consider there is more to the present situation than meets the eye. Seeing a 7 reminds you to pause and meditate. There is something to be learned. It can enhance your ceremony to incorporate 7 of anything in your design.

Numerology Code Journaling

- *When do I find myself standing in judgment of myself or others?*
- *Where can I work smarter, not harder at life?*
- *Am I willing to let go of attitudes that keep me isolated and disconnected because of fear or judgmental attitudes in the energy of the Leo Full Moon in order to create a more personal and spiritual fulfillment?*

LEO FULL MOON CEREMONY
Devic Fire

This ceremony connects you with with the enchanted realm of the devic kingdom (fAiries, elves and tree spirits). Amplify your connection with unlimited possibilities through this Fire ceremony. This is an ideal ceremony for a campout, sleepover or weekend retreat.

BEFORE YOU BEGIN GATHERING TOOLS, SAY THE FULL MOON INVOCATION FOUND ON PAGE XX.

Step One: Selecting Tools

Set up a Full Moon wishing area in a quiet space without distractions. Ideally you can do this outdoors, but a private space inside works too. Refer to the corresponding elements in the section above to select your tools. We suggest incorporating at least one tool per element (Fire, Earth, Air, Water), as well as a journal to write your intentions and responses to the journal prompts. You'll want to have a couple of sticks for this ceremony - hand-picked from nature or you could purchase popsicle sticks or wooden skewers.

Step Two: Sticks & Stones

Light some incense or a stick of palo santo. Gather your sticks and Full Moon crystals. Next, dab a few drops of any of the Leo essential oils on your hands and then rub the sticks and stones with the oils.

Say: *I am activating the energy of the Earth and calling in the nature spirits of the Devic (fAiry) realm in the highest light to come play.*

Step Three: Clarity

Once your sticks and stones are lightly coated with essential oils, close your eyes, take three deep inhalations and exhalations, noticing the sensations in your physical body as the aroma of the oils activates the energy of the sticks and stones.

Ask the Devic realm for any guidance on the nature of your current limiting beliefs and behaviors.

Say: *Devic Realm, show me what is holding me back from expressing my highest, brightest light in this lifetime.*

Take as much time as you need to meditate and listen for clarity. If your mind starts to wander, come back to your breath and the sensations in your physical body.

Step Four: Write it Out

Once your meditation is complete, cut strips of paper in enough strips to pair with the sticks. Now, on each piece of paper write the following:

It is my intention that I am willing to let go of _____. And so it is.

This is an optimal time to write any additional wishes, the Leo Full Moon Intention, and the Leo Full Moon Healing Invocation.

Step Five: Bind It

Roll each individual intention paper around a stick, tying a string around the stick to bind the paper securely around the stick. Repeat this for each intention.

Step Six: Pick Up Sticks

Gather all of your intention sticks in your hands. Close your eyes.

Say: *I activate the power of the Leo Full Moon to transmute the lower vibrations of my limiting beliefs and behaviors into pure, positive potential.*

Drop the intention sticks on the ground allowing them to scatter. Intuitively place your crystals on the outside of the sticks wherever you feel called to place them.

Step Seven: Clear The Limitations

Using your feather, wave it over the intention sticks and stones.

Say: *My heart is willing. My head is willing. My body is willing. I let go of the past. I am the present.* Repeat this the same number of times as intention sticks you have.

Step Eight: Leo Moonlight Transformation

Leave the intention sticks and crystals out for three days and nights under the Leo Full Moonlight. If you cannot leave your materials outside, you can gather them up and place them in a window for the three days and nights. Don't fret about the placement. Trust that you have invoked the magic necessary to activate and transform the intentions with your energy, belief and intention.

Step Nine: Ashes to Ashes (optional)

After the third night, gather the sticks and crystals. Put the activated crystals in your pocket or next to you on the ground. Restate the Full Moon Invocation **(Design insert pages** - refer to pp) to open sacred space. Now that the energy is activated and cleared, if you have a Fireplace, Firepit or safe place to burn your intention sticks, it is time to transmute the energies. Once you have created a Fire, safely add each intention stick to the flames. With every intention stick you burn:

Say: *Devic Realm and Fire spirits, accept my offering, purify my presence and transfer the peace that passes all understanding. And so it is.*

Option: If you cannot or do not wish to burn your intention sticks, you can find a wooded place outdoors to discard the sticks. Throw them out into the woods one by one stating the phrase above. Remember: it is the belief and intention behind the ceremony that creates the magic. If you intend to create sacred space, it is sacred space.

Step Ten: Closing Sacred Space

It is important to seal the energy after any ceremony. Refer to **page xx** for our suggestion on closing sacred space, or say your personalized closing prayers.

MAKING IT PERSONAL

Moon Musings

- Amanda

The Leo Full Moon always calls me to action in recognizing where I am playing it small. My North Node is in Leo (the direction of soul growth), thus my South Node (what is familiar or what my soul has mastered) is in Aquarius.

This is the Full Moon where I look at how I limit my inner light and let go of any behaviors (specifically Aquarian ones) that limit my soul's expression in this lifetime. Here are a few moon musings from previous Leo Full Moons:

- It is my intention that I naturally let go of self-limiting attitudes and behaviors that keep me playing small. I embrace my inner sunlight and passions.
- I am healing intellectual disassociation, alienation and over-identification through a willingness to be vulnerable and bold in my communications.
- My gifts are intended to be shared with the world in this lifetime. I am grateful for my abilities and generously share them with others.
- When I share my light wholeheartedly, healing happens. Joy flows to and through me each and everyday.
- Letting go of insecurities happens when I courageously express my true self and allow my passions to be seen.
- I detox all attitudes and beliefs that I am not enough. I am fulfilled. I am abundant.
- I am seeded from the Divine. I am grateful for each and every breath.
- May the love of the Universe transform any pain or suffering into pure joy.

Best Wishes

- Tiffany

The Full Moon in Leo hits in my 8th or 9th house depending on the degree of the Moon. So sometimes I add elements relating to shared resources (8th house) or philosophy and publishing (9th house). Here are a few wishes I have used on previous Leo Full Moons:

- I am no longer afraid to shine, and to be the star of my own life.
- I am deeply bonded to myself, and experience self-love as strength.
- I enjoy engaging my North Node in Leo, and having fun with life.
- I take heart-centered action through leadership: I no longer spend time and energy with disloyal people.
- I belong. Any codependency is replaced with healthy interdependency.
- I am healing my broken heart, and am willing to love again.
- I operate from a frequency of attraction rather than promotion.
- Above all, help me set aside what I think I know, and what I think I want, so that the Divine can flow through me. May I be of service to God and my fellows.

Virgo full Moon

WHEN THE FULL MOON IS IN VIRGO

When the Full Moon falls in the Earth sign of Virgo, it's time to look back over your harvest. Be proud of your hard work, and make a gratitude list. You might be called to clean house, and organize the details of life. This is the perfect Moon to find solutions, get grounded, and find a sense of completion. This is the Moon of the practical thinker, the helper, and the herbalist. It's time to bang the drum of reasonability and move forward with a new perspective.

Virgo is the sixth sign of the zodiac and is represented by the Virgin. It is an Earth sign, ruled by Mercury and Chiron.

Positive (High) Vibes of the Virgo New Moon

(Set intentions for closure or completion in these areas)

Clearing clutter and organizing the details of life
Trusting the process
Blending the old with the new
Finalizing procedures
Finding gratitude in all you have done
Resolving any loose ends with integrity
Finding practical solutions
Completing any service work that may have been draining
Being open to receiving constructive criticism in order to refine your life

Challenging (Low) Vibes of the Virgo New Moon

(What you might intend to remove)

Judgmental or overly critical attitudes
Analysis paralysis
Inefficiency; getting stuck in the details
Inability to see the bigger picture

In Health, Virgo Governs

(Areas of the body where you might wish for healing)

Kidneys
Intestines
Abdomen
Solar Plexus (Manipura Chakra)
Throat Chakra (Vishudha Chakra)

Sample Wishes for the Full Moon in Virgo

- I am quick to forgive others and myself.
- I am willing to put an end to analysis paralysis; it's easier for me to make decisions than ever before.
- I am organized physically, mentally, emotionally, and spiritually.
- All overly critical thoughts and judgments are now removed from me.
- I find a sense of completion with XYZ project, knowing I've given it my level best.

Virgo Full Moon Intention

I surrender over-thinking, getting stuck in the details, and rigidity with myself and others. When I let go of excess, I create sustainability. Stability, efficiency, and consistency come naturally to me.

Virgo Full Moon Healing Invocation

I experience organization and precision while feeling confident in the quality of my delivery.

Word to the Wise

When the Moon is in Virgo, you are likely feeling practical and grounded. Depending on your personal constituency and situation, you may enjoy the security and stability the Earth energy provides. But if things are feeling dense, fixed, or even stuck, you can incorporate elements from the opposite sign throughout the day to balance things out. The opposite sign of Virgo is the Water sign Pisces. Consider Water-related activities to encourage fluidity and motion: taking baths, drinking tea, making spritzes, using herbal sprays and tinctures, swimming in hot springs or a lake. It can be useful to combine the steadfastness of your intentions (Earth) with the flexibility of trusting providence to flow in at divine right timing (Water).

Working with Corresponding Elements

We suggest using one or more items of your choice from each element when designing your ceremony. Use as many or as few as you like.

VIRGO **Fire** items: Candles + Smoke

- Green and gray candles - giving
- Earthy scented candles, herbal bundles, or incense:
- Dried herbal bouquet - natural love
    - Thyme - stability
    - Sage - purification
    - Rosemary - healing

VIRGO **Earth** items: Crystals + Stones

- Amethyst - anti-anxiety
- Chrysocolla - Earth connection
- Moss Agate - peace

VIRGO **Air** items: Intentions + Mantras

- Any personal wishes you want to make in the areas Virgo governs + the High Vibe Aspects of Virgo
- Virgo Full Moon Intention
- Virgo Full Moon Healing Invocation

ARIES **Water** items: Essential Oils + Flower Essences

- Chamomile - serenity
- Grapefruit - kindness
- Sandalwood - spirituality

VIRGO FULL MOON NUMEROLOGY

There are many ways to incorporate numerology when formulating your ceremony. You can find numbers to work with in the degree of the sign, the date, the hour you conduct the ceremony, etc. The Full Moon Numerology Empowerment Code is a special formula developed by Amanda Rieger Green, MPH at Wise Skies. We like to think of this as part of our secret sauce. We

use this number to find synchronicities as well as journaling on the day of the New Moon.

Virgo Full Moon Numerology Empowerment Code = 9

Numbers have power. We add the numbers that correlate with the Sun sign and the Moon sign, to create a unique code to use in ceremonies. During the Full Moon, the Sun and the Moon appear in opposite zodiac signs. That means each one is assigned a number according to the Moon's zodiac sign and it's opposite.

The Wise Skies Formula:
Virgo Numerology Code = 6
Pisces Numerology Code = 12
Sun in Pisces (12) + Moon in Virgo (6) = 18
Reduce it down to a single digit: 1+8 = 9

The "9" Empowerment Code brings up a sense of urgency, perfectionism, and self-sacrificing tendencies. Notice when you see a 9 today: it's a reminder to stay calm and collected. Seeing a 9 reminds you to pause and be present. You don't have to spread yourself too thin, nor do it all yourself, nor do it all today. It can enhance your ceremony to incorporate 9 of anything in your design.

Numerology Code Journaling

- *Do I set unreasonable expectations for myself and others?*
- *Am I willing to let go of unreasonable expectations or unrealistic ideals in the energy of the Virgo Full Moon in order to create more peace and trust in the present moment?*

VIRGO FULL MOON CEREMONY
House Cleaning of the Heart

This ceremony offers you a window of time to reset the energy of your home, mind, energy, and heart. You have an opportunity to recast a solid foundation in any aspect of your life that has some cobwebs or old energy milling around.

BEFORE YOU BEGIN GATHERING TOOLS, SAY THE FULL MOON INVOCATION FOUND ON PAGE XX.

Step One: Selecting Tools

Set up a Full Moon wishing area in a quiet space without distractions. Ideally you can do this outdoors, but a private space inside works too. Refer to the corresponding elements in the section above to select your tools. We suggest incorporating at least one tool per element (Fire, Earth, Air, Water), as well as a journal to write your intentions and responses to the journal prompts. You'll also want to make or purchase an herbal bundle or sage wand.

Step Two: Clean House

When the Full Moon is exact (or a few hours after exact), light a green or gray candle. This is an optimal time to write wishes, intentions, or healing invocations that correspond with Virgo energy.

Take a moment to center yourself by slowing your breath. Close your eyes, and deeply inhale and exhale for three cycles through your nose. Invite your eyes to open, grab your journal, and write these clearing intentions:

MENTAL CLEARING: I allow myself to clear all mental clutter, outdated beliefs, and critical thoughts that limit my value (insert thoughts):_____.

EMOTIONAL CLEARING: I organically process all lower vibrational emotions with clarity, trust, and confidence. I am currently processing (insert emotions): _____.

PHYSICAL CLEARING: I recognize and honor aspects of my physical body that are stressed, weakened, or not functioning at optimal capacity. I allow for the healing of (insert what you want to be healed physically):_____.

SPIRITUAL CLEARING: I trust my Higher Self to guide and direct me with unconditional love and compassion. I allow any blockages to my conscious contact with my Higher Self and Higher Power will be dissolved with pure love and divine light.

Step Three: Activation

Dab a few drops of essential oils in your palms and rub them together vigorously. Now, bring your palms up to your nose, inhaling deeply. Visualize a white liquid light clearing your mind, body and spirit. Think and feel "clear."

Tap your heart chakra using your thumb, first, and second finger. Repeatedly tap the heart chakra while saying "clear" for three to four breath cycles. Then do the same over your third eye, throat, and crown chakra. Tap anywhere on the body you feel intuitively guided to stir and clear the energy.

Now, dab some oil on your intentions. Place the intentions out under the Virgo Full Moon light. Set a few of crystals on top of your intentions to charge under the moonlight for 3 nights. You can always do this inside near a moonlit window if you need to; it's the intention and action that creates the energy and activation.

Step Four: Smudging and Herbal Blessing

If you created a dried herbal bouquet 6 months prior during the Virgo New Moon, it's now time to infuse the energy of your intentions and yourself with the charged up herbal essences. If you didn't make a bouquet then, or didn't keep it - that's ok! You can use a sage wand or herbal bouquet from the store.

Carefully light the herbal wand or bundle, creating an aromatic smoke. Wave the smoke over your intentions and crystals. Then wave the smoke over yourself from head to toe. This is called smudging. Repeat the entire smudging process over intentions, crystals, and yourself 3 times. While you smudge:

Say: *I am responsible for my energy. Any lower vibrations are transmuted into divine light and intelligence. All aspects of me are here now, clean and clear.*

Step Five: Crystal Power

After the 3 nights of charging, gather your intentions and crystals. You may wish to burn or bury the intentions. The act of putting the intentions into another element assists the transmutation process.

Carry the crystals with you for the next two weeks (in your pocket, next to your bed, in your purse, on your desk, in the car, wherever you like). Each time you look at the crystals, consider that they are living energies assisting you with your wishes. Thank them for their innate intelligence from the Earth and their grounding energies.

Step Six: Closing Sacred Space

It is important to seal the energy after any ceremony. Refer to **page xx** for our suggestion on closing sacred space, or say your personalized closing prayers.

Full Moon House Clearing.

We love to clean our houses on the New Moon, but the Virgo Full Moon also has special purging and cleansing energies. Add a few drops of essential oils to your mop Water, put a few drops around your door, and on the four corners of your bed. Read more about house clearing in the Cancer New Moon ceremony, and in *Numerology for your Home*, by Amanda Rieger Green, MPH or download our guide at www.WiseSkiesAdvice.com.

MAKING IT PERSONAL

Moon Musings

- Amanda

The Virgo Full Moon is usually an energy where I invite spring cleaning. My natal Jupiter and Venus fall in Virgo and are usually triggered during this energy, so naturally, I embrace a house cleaning that focuses on anything presently limiting my abundance or ability to experience love (giving and receiving). Here are a few moon musings from previous Virgo Full Moons:

- I let go of anything limiting my ability to experience abundance in every aspect of my life.

- I trust my worth, value, and capacity to experience happiness and joy, while taking practical action in cleaning out anything blocking my flow.
- I let go of any inefficient processes or distractions in order to create greater efficiency, effectiveness and ease, one day (and task) at a time.
- I recognize that being busy or overwhelmed is not directly proportional to my abundance. I open my heart to love and balance.
- Health and well-being come naturally to me each and everyday. I crave high vibrational actions and environments.
- Detoxing self-critical and judgmental behaviors organically detox through my body, creating space for more love, kindness and peace.
- I practice healthy self-care in order to be of maximum service to the multiverse.

Best Wishes

- Tiffany

The Full Moon in Virgo hits in my 9th or 10th house depending on the degree of the New Moon. So sometimes I add elements relating to my big adventure, publishing, or worldview (9th house) or career and public standing (10th house) issues. Here are a few wishes I have used on previous Virgo New Moons:

- I'm good right here right now.
- I enjoy feeling a sense of completion with the current publishing schedule, knowing that we have produced books that leave the world a better place.
- Anything blocking or limiting me in my health and vitality is now purged and gone.
- I am service-oriented while keeping healthy boundaries. When I help others, it helps me.
- The more organized and clean my house is, the more clarity I gain.
- I love tapping into the Wise Woman knowledge of our elders and access Earth magic through the feminine divine connection.
- I enjoy learning more about the garden to make homemade teas, and herbal remedies that cleanse and clear my kidneys, intestines, and abdomen.
- Above all, help me set aside what I think I know, and what I think I want, so that the Divine can flow through me. May I be of service to God and my fellows.

Libra full Moon

WHEN THE FULL MOON IS IN LIBRA

When the Full Moon falls in the Air sign of Libra, you can expect to feel supported, or to want to feel supported. There might be some indecision or tackiness in the Airwaves if the Moon is negatively aspected. But it's also possible you might notice more beauty, balance, and harmony. This is the perfect Moon to redecorate, set partnership intentions, and explore areas that benefit from multiple perspectives. It's a Moon to be mindful of treating others as you wish to be treated. This is the Moon of the true partner, and the interior decorator. It's time to bang the drum of friendship and look at the world with fAirness in your eyes.

Libra is the seventh sign in the zodiac and is represented by the Scales. It is an Air sign, ruled by Venus.

Positive (High) Vibes of the Libra Full Moon

(Set intentions for closure or completion in these areas)

Finding a sense of completion through fAir justice
Recognizing areas that have been unbalanced
Finding closure with any unhealthy partnerships
Seeking all perspectives to find a win-win
Allowing forgiveness
Putting an end to any dishonest or inauthentic behaviors

Challenging (Low) Vibes of the Libra Full Moon

(What you might intend to remove)

People-pleasing
Indecision
Unhealthy compromise
Two-faced

In Health, Libra Governs

(Areas of the body where you might wish for healing)

Skin
Belly button
Waist
Heart Chakra (Anahata Chakra)

Sample Wishes for the Full Moon in Libra

- I am decisive and take action without hesitation or procrastination.
- Discernment happens naturally.
- I am honest in my communication with myself and others.
- I naturally express my thoughts, feelings and needs in the present moment with authenticity and clarity.
- I easily recognize emotional imbalance and process my feelings in healthy ways.

Libra Full Moon Intention

I easily let go of people-pleasing and indecisive behaviors, allowing a greater sense of balance, well-being, and love to fill both my head and heart.

Libra Full Moon Healing Invocation

Peace and ease flow naturally to and through my being. I bring light onto the planet through all of my relationships.

Word to the Wise

When the Moon is in Libra, it's possible you are seeking fAirness, balance, and beauty. Depending on your personal constituency and situation, you may enjoy the endless options provided under an Air-Moon. But if things are feeling too indecisive and scattered, you can incorporate elements from the opposite sign throughout the day to balance things out. The opposite sign of Libra is Aries. Consider contemplative yoga or something that combines thought (Air) with action (Fire). Combining Air and Fire elements assists you in transmuting your intentions into the highest and brightest frequencies.

Working with Corresponding Elements

We suggest using one or more items of your choice from each element when designing your ceremony. Use as many or as few as you like.

LIBRA **Fire** items: Candles + Smoke

- Purple, pastel, and pink candles - divinity
- Floral scented candles, herbal bundles, or incense:
  - Rose - love
  - Lavender - illumination

LIBRA **Earth** items: Crystals + Stones

- Apatite - decisiveness
- Fluorite - mental acuity
- Chevron Amethyst - wisdom

LIBRA **Air** items: Intentions + Mantras

- Any personal wishes you want to make in the areas Libra governs + the High Vibe Aspects of Libra
- Libra Full Moon Intention
- Libra Full Moon Healing Invocation

LIBRA **Water** items: Essential Oils + Flower Essences

- Rose - love
- Lavender - calm
- Geranium -compassion
- Ylang Ylang - harmonizing

LIBRA FULL MOON NUMEROLOGY

There are many ways to incorporate numerology when formulating your ceremony. You can find numbers to work with in the degree of the sign, the date, the hour you conduct the ceremony, etc. The Full Moon Numerology Empowerment Code is a special formula developed by Amanda Rieger Green, MPH at Wise Skies. We like to think of this as part of our secret sauce. We use this number to find synchronicities as well as journaling on the day of the New Moon.

Libra Full Moon Numerology Empowerment Code = 8

Numbers have power. We add the numbers that correlate with the Sun sign and the Moon sign, to create a unique code to use in ceremonies. During the Full Moon, the Sun and the Moon appear in opposite zodiac signs. That means each one is assigned a number according to the Moon's zodiac sign and it's opposite.

The Wise Skies Formula:
Libra Numerology = 7
Aries Numerology Code = 1
Sun in Aries (1) + Moon in Libra (7) = 8

The "8" Empowerment Code helps us gain awareness of ego and stubbornness. Notice when you see an 8 today: it's a reminder to stay open-minded to opportunities. Seeing an 8 reminds you to pause and trust the process. It can enhance your ceremony to incorporate 8 of anything in your design.

Numerology Code Journaling

- *Where do I find that my motives are driven by ego rather than purpose?*
- *Am I willing to surrender to something greater than me and trust the process in the energy of the Libra Full Moon, in order to feel more my heart and head more fully aligned?*

LIBRA FULL MOON CEREMONY
Chakra Bath

This ceremony is a highly activated ritual that balances the chakras while also clearing your auric field, and helping you find greater resonance with your emotional navigation system. This ceremony is ideal for healing and aligning your energy.

Be mindful of your dreams tonight. Chakra baths can be very powerful in triggering and unlocking intelligence or memories from your cells and DNA. Journal any dreams you recall over the next three days. Namaste!

BEFORE YOU BEGIN GATHERING TOOLS, SAY THE FULL MOON INVOCATION FOUND ON PAGE XX.

Step One: Selecting Tools

Set up a Full Moon wishing area in a quiet space without distractions. Ideally you can do this outdoors, but a private space inside works too. Refer to the corresponding elements in the section above to select your tools. We suggest incorporating at least one tool per element (Fire, Earth, Air, Water), as well as a journal to write your intentions and responses to the journal prompts. You'll also want a floral tea for this ceremony (we like rose, chamomile, or lavender).

Step Two: Tea Time

Brew your choice of floral tea. Why floral? Flowery teas help conjure the beautiful grounding energy of Mother Nature. Option: add your favorite nut milk and agave for an even sweeter experience.

Step Three: Spiritual Support

Open the ceremony by sipping your tea, lighting a rose or lavender scented candle, and placing one or more crystals on a table nearby. Breathe slowly through your nose and begin to relax.

Say: *I call in my spirit guides, angels, ancestors, spirit animals and highest version of myself. Please work with me in the highest vibrations of light and love. I open sacred space for pure, positive illumination.*

Imagine that there are four guides in a circle around you. As you meditate and breathe, see their faces, energy, and presence. Look around the circle, connecting with each of them. Thank them for inspiring your enlightenment and holding sacred space in the quantum field for you.

Take a few minutes to breathe, meditate, and feel the love of being spiritually supported.

Step Four: Remove Obstacles

When you are comfortable with feeling the presence of (or even just the idea of) your spirit guides, ask them to reveal any blocks, limitations, or outdated karmic patterns that are weighing on you at this time. Listen for their responses. Trust the thoughts, feelings, insights, colors, imagery, sensations and more that come to you - these responses are your answers. You don't have to know or understand all of the information you are receiving. Trust that healing intelligence is being transmitted into your cells.

When you are ready, ask your support team to assist you in removing any obstacles that limit you from your highest purpose.

Say: *I am willing to put down anything heavy or burdensome that is holding me back from the best version of my life. I am ready to shift into higher realms of consciousness and being. Thank you for your help.*

Take a moment to silently thank your spirit guides for assisting you and for their unconditional, evolutionary healing energy. If you would like to repeat the exercise, envisioning going around the circle with each guide present, please do so.

Step Five: Set Intentions

Once you feel a sense of completion, journal any thoughts, insights, and revelations. Next, begin to consider how you would like to incorporate any new knowledge into intentions. Reminder: the optimal time to write down intentions is when the Moon is exactly Full, or within the following few hours of it being Full (not before).

Step Six: Bath Time

Draw a nice bath (a shower is optional too) and create sacred space for yourself for the next 15-30 minutes. Drop your Libra Full Moon crystals into the tub for grounding and energetic integrity. Ask the stones to stabilize and clear any unhealthy or unnatural electromagnetic frequencies harming your energy field.

Say: *I am the Magician/Priestess. This space is purified and the Water is ready for ultimate conductivity.*

Infuse your bath with essential oils. Add a few drops to your Water, inhaling the fragrance and possibly adding a few drops to the back of your neck and behind your ears.

As you inhale, think: *The oxygen is healing, and purifying me.*

As you exhale, think: *My cells are clean, my body returns to full vitality and strength.*

Repeat this for as many breath cycles you like.

Step Seven: Chakra Alignment

Begin to meditate on your intentions. Which one is the most important to you right now?

Visualize all the colors of the rainbow, one by one as you read each of the chakra mantras out loud and visualize each chakra center spinning freely.

Red: Root Chakra

I am rooted. I am grounded. I am safe. I am secure. I accept my body as a beautiful temple of biological intelligence. I honor my physical existence.

Orange: Sacral Chakra

I am in emotional balance. I feel emotional well-being. I honor and process my feelings with optimal integrity and courage. I am divine creativity. I honor my sensuality and sexuality. I accept my emotional intelligence as both human and divine.

Yellow: Solar Plexus Chakra

I AM. I trust my innate wisdom. I digest and process life optimally. I accept my I Am present in all aspects of my life as both human and divine.

Green and Pink: Heart Chakra

I am the essence of unconditional love. I am worthy of giving and receiving unconditional love. I am compassionate. I honor all experiences as opportunities to express more love and more compassion, never less. I accept the vibration of unconditional love to flow to and through me freely.

Blue: Throat Chakra

I am authentic. I speak words of the highest vibrations of love and acceptance to myself and others. I express myself with clarity, assurance, and truth. I accept and honor the power of my words to materialize an abundant reality.

Indigo: Third Eye Chakra

I am interconnected to my innermost being, essence, and intelligence. I know the universe within and feel it in the core of my being. I trust my innate Higher Self to guide and direct my thoughts and actions for the greater good.

Violet and Diamond Light: Crown Chakra

I am open and connected to and through the cosmos. The light of the Universe flows to and through me. I am an extraordinary spirit having a human experience. And so it is.

Which color stands out to you the most? Trust that the predominant color you receive during meditation has the healing properties you need to purge what is not needed in your field.

Take as much time as you need to relax, integrate, and feel the frequencies transmitted through your chakra system, your guides, and your Higher Self.

Step Eight: Easy Does It

After your bath or shower and chakra healing meditation, you can massage essential oils onto your skin, around joints and tense spots (be careful not to get them into your eyes or mouth). Option: mix the oils with jojoba, almond or coconut oil.

You may want to continue writing about anything that came to mind while you were reciting the chakra mantras.

Step Nine: Closing Sacred Space

It is important to seal the energy after any ceremony. Refer to **page xx** for our suggestion on closing sacred space, or say your personalized closing prayers.

MAKING IT PERSONAL

Moon Musings

- *Amanda*

The Full Moon in Libra is always a huge opportunity for me to let go of innate behaviors and attitudes that inhibit peace in my reality. Why? My natal Sun and Moon are in Libra as well as a host of other planets. This Full Moon usually triggers the present insecurities that I'm needing to detox in order to find greater clarity, balance, harmony and ultimately, personal/spiritual evolution. Here are a few moon musings from previous Libra Full Moons:

- I let go of any ego-based fears and perceptions that limit my serenity, each and everyday.
- I stand in my truth and trust the discernment of my mind, body, and spirit. I communicate authentically in all aspects of my life.
- Sacrificing my individuality in relationships feels unnatural. I embrace interdependence in all relationships.
- Peace, ease, and serenity are natural states of being in my nervous system, mind and consciousness.
- Higher levels of conscious and awareness come through transcending my ego and shifting into my highest perspective.
- Recognizing the symptoms of emotional imbalance comes naturally. I take thoughtful action and recenter peacefully.

Love prevails.

Best Wishes

- *Tiffany*

The Full Moon in Libra hits in my 10th or 11th house depending on the degree of the Moon. So sometimes I add elements relating to career (10th) or community (11th) related themes. Here are a few wishes I have used on previous Libra Full Moons:

- I respond with calmness, I no longer need to react.
- I let go of unhealthy relationships, making room for healthy connections.
- I stand up for myself, not against the other person.
- I recalibrate my energy to the frequency of compatibility and balance.
- I crave only foods that are healthy for my body and enhance my life force energy.
- Above all, help me set aside what I think I know, and what I think I want, so that the Divine can flow through me. May I be of service to God and my fellows.

Scorpio full Moon

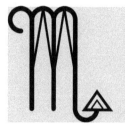

WHEN THE FULL MOON IS IN SCORPIO

When the Full Moon falls in the Water sign of Scorpio, things can feel intense. Like the hermit or priestess card in the tarot, it is normal to want to have personal time right now. This is the perfect Moon to wrap up an old research project, to set an intention around self-development, or to overcome something deep. This is the Moon of the alchemist, the sensualist, and the power player. It's time to bang the drum of self-transcendence and look at the world with intuitive eyes.

Scorpio is the eighth sign in the zodiac and is represented by the Scorpion. It is a Water sign, ruled by Mars and Pluto.

Positive (High) Vibes of the Scorpio Full Moon

(Set intentions for closure or completion in these areas)

The ability to execute or finish projects
Transcending, growing, and using metaphysical self-discovery tools
Closure on unhealthy obsessions
Overcoming addictions
Finding closure from emotional vampires
Leaning on spiritual resources
Finding committed connection with an intimate partner
Healing power struggles and finding your personal power
Cashing in on financial pathways through shared resources

Challenging (Low) Vibes of the Scorpio Full Moon

(What you might intend to remove)

Jealousy
Resentment
Secrecy
Distrust
Revenge

In Health, Scorpio Governs

(Areas of the body where you might wish for healing)

Urinary system
Kidneys
Gallbladder
Sex organs
Elimination organs
Sacral Chakra (Svadhisthana Chakra)

Sample wishes for the Full Moon in Scorpio

I overcome any dark feelings of jealousy, revenge, and anger.
I take time to cleanse and purge unhealthy obsessions.
I appreciate my resourcefulness, and trust that I will always be divinely guided.
I love playing with magic, meditation, prayer, and transcendence to shift into a new version of myself that I'm proud of.
I'm willing to let the hardest part be over.
I appreciate a sense of completion and closure.

Scorpio Full Moon Intention

I crave healthy attitudes, behaviors, and experiences, and inherently choose my actions with integrity and transparency.

Scorpio Full Moon Healing Invocation

I access my wisdom and share it compassionately with those around me.

Word to the Wise

When the Moon is in Scorpio, it's possible you are feeling intense emotions and have increased intuition. Your spidey-senses are in full swing. You may notice people are feeling passionate, or are more easily triggered. Depending on your personal constituency and situation, you may enjoy the emotional depth provided under a Water-Moon. But if things are feeling too heavy, you can incorporate elements from the opposite sign throughout the day to balance things out. The opposite sign of Scorpio is Taurus. Consider drumming, walking on the ground outside with bare feet, or visualizing roots growing through your feet to the center of the Earth in meditation. Combining Water and Earth elements assists you in anchoring your intentions with practical action to bring about desired outcomes.

Working with Corresponding Elements

We suggest using one or more items of your choice from each element when designing your ceremony. Use as many or as few as you like.

SCORPIO **Fire** items: Candles + Smoke

- Black and orange candles - passion
- Ethereal scented candles, herbal bundles, or incense:
    - Palo Santo - security
    - Cedarwood - grounding
    - Aloe - soothing

SCORPIO **Earth** items: Crystals + Stones

- Carnelian - emotional stability
- Obsidian - energetic clearing
- Peridot - magic

SCORPIO **Air** items: Intentions + Mantras

- Any personal wishes you want to make in the areas Scorpio governs + the High Vibe Aspects of Scorpio
- Scorpio Full Moon Intention
- Scorpio Full Moon Healing Invocation

SCORPIO **Water** items: Essential Oils + Flower Essences

- Ylang Ylang - balancing
- Jasmine -spirituality
- Sandalwood -sweetness

SCORPIO FULL MOON NUMEROLOGY

There are many ways to incorporate numerology when formulating your ceremony. You can find numbers to work with in the degree of the sign, the date, the hour you conduct the ceremony, etc. The Full Moon Numerology Empowerment Code is a special formula developed by Amanda Rieger Green, MPH at Wise Skies. We like to think of this as part of our secret sauce. We use this number to find synchronicities as well as journaling on the day of the New Moon.

Scorpio Full Moon Numerology Empowerment Code = 1

Numbers have power. We add the numbers that correlate with the Sun sign and the Moon sign, to create a unique code to use in ceremonies. During the Full Moon, the Sun and the Moon appear in opposite zodiac signs. That means each one is assigned a number according to the Moon's zodiac sign and it's opposite.

The Wise Skies Formula:
Taurus Numerology Code = 2
Scorpio Numerology = 8
Sun in Taurus (2) + Moon in Scorpio (8) = 10
Reduce it down to a single digit: 1+0 = 1

The "1" Empowerment Code offers insights around areas where we may be stubborn, have tunnel vision, or are being single-minded. Notice when you see a 1 today: it's a reminder to remain flexible, knowing there is always more to the story. Seeing a 1 reminds you to pause and open your heart and mind to a higher perspective. It can enhance your ceremony to incorporate 1 of anything in your design.

Numerology Code Journaling

- *Where do I feel unimaginative or overly focused on my ideas or processes?*
- *Am I willing to let go of stubborn and rigid thinking in the energy of the Scorpio Full Moon in order to create a richer, fuller life?*

SCORPIO FULL MOON CEREMONY
Medicinal Potion

In this ceremony, you will create a medicinal spray to clear your auric field and enhance your dreams and psychic insights. This ceremony is powerfully effective clearing negative energy by yourself or in a group. You can keep the magical potion, or offer it as a gift to others.

BEFORE YOU BEGIN GATHERING TOOLS, SAY THE FULL MOON INVOCATION FOUND ON PAGE XX.

Step One: Selecting Tools

Set up a Full Moon wishing area in a quiet space without distractions. Ideally you can do this outdoors, but a private space inside works too. Refer to the corresponding elements in the section above to select your tools. We suggest incorporating at least one tool per element (Fire, Earth, Air, Water), as well as a journal to write your intentions and responses to the journal prompts. You'll also want to get a lemon or lime, chai tea, and a spray bottle with a large enough opening to fit small crystals through the top.

Step Two: Prepare

Light a black or orange candle. Boil enough Water for a cup of tea and a little extra for your spray bottle to be filled ¾ full. Relax and enjoy the tea while you settle into the witchy magic of the Scorpio Full Moon. Option: put a cleared and charged crystal in your tea cup for extra infusion.

Step Three: Purify

After the extra Water has cooled, squeeze a full lemon or lime into the Water.

Say: *I purify this Water with the sweet and sour of life, knowing that there can be no light without darkness.*

Once cooled down, transfer the lemon/lime infused Water into the spray bottle.

Step Four: Crystal Magick

Add small carnelian, obsidian or peridot stones or crystals to the spray bottle. Make sure the crystals are clean and feel energetically good to you. As you drop them in:

Say: *I activate this potion with passion, purpose, focus, and truth. My motives are pure.*

Step Five: Journal

Wait for time of the Scorpio Full Moon, or within a few hours after, to write your intentions. What do you want? What are you willing to let go of in order to experience more trust, faith, openness, honesty, and clarity? Write up to ten intentions on a separate sheet of paper:

In order to receive _____ it is my intention that I willingly and naturally let go of _____. (Repeat for each intention.)

Example: In order to receive unconditional love, it is my intention that I willingly and naturally let go of unhealthy, painful relationships and take responsibility for my life.

This is also an optimal time to write any extra wishes, along with our Scorpio Full Moon intention and healing invocation if it speaks to you.

Step Six: Clear + Cleanse

Spray your auric field with the activated potion. Breathe in the aroma. Feel the clarity, peace, and tingly activation. Next, read each separate piece of paper with the intentions out loud, and spray each one with your potion.

Step Seven: Moonlight Medicine

Place the intention papers outside (or next to a window) for the next three nights, spraying them once each day. Spray once over yourself each day as well.

Option: you can keep the spray by your bed and lightly spray your pillow once each night for the next two weeks during the waning Lunar cycle. Each night ask your Higher Self to activate your dream state to help you clear and evolve into a higher, lighter, and brighter version of you.

Step Eight: Closing Sacred Space

It is important to seal the energy after any ceremony. Refer to **page xx** for our suggestion on closing sacred space, or say your personalized closing prayers.

MAKING IT PERSONAL

Moon Musings

- Amanda

The Scorpio Full Moon is an energy that usually triggers psychic insights, intensive dreams, insecurities and a whole host of "stuff" to confront. My natal Mercury, Mars and Uranus are all in Scorpio. Yes, that's a whole lot of powerful Scorpio energy. I use this Full Moon to detox fears and ego-based behaviors. Here are a few moon musings from previous Scorpio Full Moons:

- I willingly and courageously let go of insecurities, doubts, and worries, creating space for more love and light.
- I naturally identify and let go of jealousy, anger, and resentment, to be more aligned with my highest evolutionary Self.
- I naturally create divine alignment between my feelings and actions. My head and my heart are connected through a channel of peace.
- My passions and sensuality are channeled in a healthy, loving way and are vulnerably expressed with clarity, trust and truth.
- People, places and things that limit my ability to trust and feel safe organically shift from my reality in divine timing.
- Honesty with myself, others and my Higher Power comes naturally in all circumstances.

Best Wishes

- Tiffany

The Scorpio Full Moon in Scorpio hits in my 11th or 12th house depending on the degree of the Moon. So sometimes I add elements relating to friends and wishes (11th house) or subconscious desires (12th house). My natal Sun, Moon, Mercury, and Uranus are all in Scorpio - so this is a particularly magnetizing birthday-Moon for me. Here are a few wishes I have used on previous Scorpio Full Moons:

- I am selfless and powerful beyond measure in service to my highest divine vision.
- The worst is over, I'm ready to shine my fullest potential.
- I surrender all limiting beliefs about other people back to the divine, they are free to shine in their own unique God-presence and so am I.
- I enjoy working with my galactic council to cause a wave of unconditional love and awakening through my business.
- I forgive quickly, and make amends whenever necessary, keeping my side of the street as clean as possible.
- I no longer live in lack; I easily tap into the frequency of financial abundance.
- Above all, help me set aside what I think I know, and what I think I want, so that the Divine can flow through me. May I be of service to God and my fellows.

Sagittarius full Moon

WHEN THE FULL MOON IS IN SAGITTARIUS

When the Full Moon falls in the Fire sign of Sagittarius, you can expect to feel spontaneous and spirited. You might notice extra energy, including the competitive vibes of the archer. This is the perfect Moon to consider the path of responsibility, and to overcome issues around excess. This is the Moon of the philosopher, the loyal friend, and the gypsy. It's time to bang the drum of self-knowledge and look at the world with realistic optimism.

Sagittarius is the ninth sign in the zodiac and is represented by the Centaur. It is a Fire sign, ruled by Jupiter.

Positive (High) Vibes of the Sagittarius Full Moon

(Set intentions for closure or completion in these areas)

Putting an end to excess growth (overeating, drinking too much, obsessing)
Finalizing travel plans
Finishing a course or class work
Committing to a mentor or mentee
Finding a sense of completion through artistic endeavors
Being willing to no longer live in a lie
Creating an end of the day devotional activity
Making peace with friends, family, and companions
Finishing the publishing or writing process
Completing a meditation
Finding peace of mind through personal responsibility

Challenging (Low) Vibes of the Sagittarius New Moon

(What you might intend to remove)

Procrastination
Delusional thinking or overly optimistic attitudes
Over-doing things or exaggerating

Taking shortcuts
Making assumptions

In Health, Sagittarius Governs

(Areas of the body where you might wish for healing)

Hips
Thighs
Arteries
Liver
Sciatica
Solar Plexus (Manipura)

Sample Wishes for the Full Moon in Sagittarius

- I easily overcome procrastination; I have the energy, decisions, and drive to propel my life forward.
- I no longer overcommit myself; I retain my life force energy for myself and most important project.s
- I look forward to my graduation from the Masters program in health next year.

Sagittarius Full Moon Intention

I am willing to let go of unnecessary excess and overcompensation to create space for pure motivation, consistency, and whole-hearted effort. My heart is joyful.

Sagittarius Full Moon Healing Invocation

I evoke the balance of sophistication and playfulness in order to find meaning and substance.

Word to the Wise

When the Moon is in Sagittarius, you are likely feeling stir crazy and ready to get out of the house. Depending on your personal constituency and situation, you may enjoy the Fire energy. But if things are feeling too heated, you can incorporate elements from the opposite sign throughout the day to balance things out. The opposite sign of Sagittarius is the Air sign Gemini. Consider contemplative activities like a walking meditation in a labyrinth to combine action (Fire) with mindfulness (Air).

Working with Corresponding Elements

We suggest using one or more items of your choice from each element when designing your ceremony. Use as many or as few as you like.

SAGITTARIUS **Fire** items: Candles + Smoke

- Royal blue or purple candles - wisdom
- Luxurious and enriching scented candles, herbal bundles, or incense:
    - Sage - clearing
    - Peppermint - focus
    - Lavender - peace

SAGITTARIUS **Earth** items: Crystals + Stones

- Lepidolite - descriptions
- Peacock Ore - alignment
- Fire Agate - passion

SAGITTARIUS **Air** items: Intentions + Mantras

- Any personal wishes you want to make in the areas Sagittarius governs + the High Vibe Aspects of Sagittarius
- Sagittarius Full Moon Intention
- Sagittarius Full Moon Healing Invocation

SAGITTARIUS **Water** items: Essential Oils + Flower Essences

- Tea Tree - descriptions
- Lavender - peace
- Eucalyptus - trust

SAGITTARIUS FULL MOON NUMEROLOGY

There are many ways to incorporate numerology when formulating your ceremony. You can find numbers to work with in the degree of the sign, the date, the hour you conduct the ceremony, etc. The Full Moon Numerology Empowerment Code is a special formula developed by Amanda Rieger Green, MPH at Wise Skies. We like to think of this as part of our secret sauce. We use this number to find synchronicities as well as journaling on the day of the New Moon.

Sagittarius Full Moon Numerology Empowerment Code = 3

Numbers have power. We add the numbers that correlate with the Sun sign and the Moon sign, to create a unique code to use in ceremonies. During the Full Moon, the Sun and the Moon appear in opposite zodiac signs. That means each one is assigned a number according to the Moon's zodiac sign and it's opposite.

The Wise Skies Formula:
Gemini Numerology Code = 3
Sagittarius Numerology Code = 9
Sun in Gemini (3) + Moon in Sagittarius (9) = 12
Reduce it down to a single digit: 1+2 = 3

The "3" Empowerment Code invites us to consider when we might say yes, but mean no. Notice when you see a 3 today: it's a reminder to ask yourself what's best for your highest good at this time. Where can you be creatively authentic to yourself? Seeing a 3 reminds you to pause and be mindful before making any moves. It can enhance your ceremony to incorporate e of anything in your design.

Numerology Code Journaling

- *When do I say "yes" when I really mean "no" or "I don't know?"*
- *When do I find myself resentful of over-committing myself and feeling stretched thin or depleted?*
- *Under the Sagittarius Full Moon, am I willing to let go of any people-pleasing or conditioned behaviors in order to honor my inner truth and practice authenticity?*

SAGITTARIUS FULL MOON CEREMONY
Divine Insight

This ceremony uses the art of divination with an oracle or tarot deck alongside a Full Moon shower to wash away unwanted energy. This ceremony will powerfully close out anything that prevents you from living purposefully. You can also do this ceremony at the end of a year to seal the year's lessons, when you're finalizing a business deal, or finding completion in a relationship. When we mindfully work to bring closure to any aspect of our life, we simultaneously prepare sacred space for something new to richly grow.

BEFORE YOU BEGIN GATHERING TOOLS, SAY THE FULL MOON INVOCATION FOUND ON PAGE XX.

Step One: Selecting Tools

Set up a Full Moon wishing area in a quiet space without distractions. Ideally you can do this outdoors, but a private space inside works too. Refer to the corresponding elements in the section above to select your tools. We suggest incorporating at least one tool per element (Fire, Earth, Air, Water), as well as a journal to write your intentions and responses to the journal prompts.

Step Two: Conscious Connection

Find a comfortable place to sit. Open the essential oil(s), and deeply breathe them in to center and ground yourself. Imagine that you have roots in your feet that are shooting down to the center of the Earth. Visualize a beautiful, pure, smoky quartz crystal at the Earth's core. Envision your roots wrapping around that crystal and simultaneously offering and receiving the energy and infinite intelligence of the crystal that represents the Living Core Knowledge of the Earth.

Create some Fire with your breath by simply breathing in and out in rapid intervals—with your mouth open in an "o" shape. Imagine that you are giving Fire to the Earth with each exhale and purifying your body, mind and spirit with the Fire you draw back up from the Earth. After twelve breath cycles:

Say: *The flame of divine intelligence is ignited within me.*

When you are ready, light the candle. Leave it burning for the next steps.

Step Three: Creating Magick

Shuffle the card deck several times, then cut the deck in half. Place it in front of you, both sides facing down. Place crystals on or around the deck.

Say*: This deck is clear. And so it is.*

Step Four: Fire gazing

Gaze into the flame of the candle. Breathe in and out of your nose for three cycles. Shuffle the deck again. As you shuffle,

Say: *Show me what needs to come to a close in this Sagittarius Full Moon energy.*

If this is a personal deck that you are familiar with, you can create any spread you like. If you are new to playing with oracle decks, we suggest a simple three card spread that indicates: what happened in the past, what is happening now, what will happen in the future if nothing else changes.

Step Five: Divination

Write any insights and wisdom you received from the card reading. Review the Sagittarius Full Moon intention and suggested writing prompts. Get clear on what cycle is ending for you personally. Get curious about the relationship between your personal cycles and the universal cycles. Are there any similarities between the cycles in the world and your personal cycles?

Settle into a space where you can write up to ten intentions. We suggest writing intentions at the time the Full Moon is exact or within a few hours following.

Step Six: Cleansing and Clearing

Take a purifying shower to rinse off. After showering, scrub your body from head to toe with epsom or Himalayan sea salt.

Say: *I am cleansing and clearing out all lower vibrational energies that do not serve my highest good. Any thoughts, feelings, or energy that is not mine are offered back to the Earth to be transmuted into pure, positive light. All aspects of me are here now. I am pure, healthy, and vibrant.*

Step Seven: Grounding

Once you have towelled off, use your essential oil by dabbing them behind your neck and ears, along your spine and on the soles of your feet. Stand still like a mountain. Breathe.

Repeat the imagination exercise from the beginning (while standing), imagining that roots are shooting down into the ground. Breathe in and out imagining the breath of Fire as you are one with the Earth. Wrap your roots around the Earth's wise central crystal.

Step Eight: Activate Intentions

Once you find a sense of completion, fold the paper with your intentions on it and hide them in a secret place for three nights. On the third day, read your intentions out loud, burn them carefully over your kitchen sink so the ashes land in a bowl. Then pour Water over the ashes. Offer the Watery ashes to any healthy plant that is growing in or near your home.

Step Nine: Closing Sacred Space

It is important to seal the energy after any ceremony. Refer to **page xx** for our suggestion on closing sacred space, or say your personalized closing prayers.

MAKING IT PERSONAL

Moon Musings

- Amanda

The Full Moon in Sagittarius usually hits my 6th house (work & day to day responsibilities), plus my natal Neptune is in Sagittarius. I usually focus on anything that that creates delusion, inefficiency, or unrealistic perspectives in my day to day work/life balance and processes. This is also a Full Moon where I let go of my usual intensive behaviors and embrace more joy, adventure, travel and freedom! Here are a few moon musings from previous Sagittarius New Moons:

- I let go of anything that limits my personal and spiritual freedom, each and everyday.

- I naturally find efficient processes and solutions in my work and responsibilities.
- My to-do lists are completed with joy, efficiency, effectiveness, and optimal outcomes. I let go of perfectionistic attitudes and behaviors and trust that I am enough (and do enough) one day at a time.
- My reality is abundant and filled with wonder, awe and clarity.
- Life class always amazes me through a prolific unfolding of consciousness, synchronicities and inspiration. I am grateful to be a conscious co-creation on Earth in this time-space reality.
- I value my life and the opportunities for cosmic, exponential evolution in this lifetime.

Best Wishes

- Tiffany

The Full Moon in Sagittarius hits in my 12th or 1st house depending on the degree of the Moon. So sometimes I add elements relating to subconscious desires (12th house) or ego/self (1st house). My natal Mars and Neptune are in Sagittarius - and I have Sag-rising. I usually experience extra energy and drive to pursue big dreams this time of year. Here are a few wishes I have used on previous Sagittarius New Moons:

- Nothing gets in the way of my life's biggest adventures.
- It's ok to say goodbye to people, places, and things that are limiting my growth.
- I radically explore ways to be active with putting an end to things that hurt the Earth and our humanity.
- Above all, help me set aside what I think I know, and what I think I want, so that the Divine can flow through me. May I be of service to God and my fellows.

Capricorn full Moon

WHEN THE FULL MOON IS IN CAPRICORN

When the Full Moon falls in the Earth sign of Capricorn, you can expect to feel ambitious, intuitive, and driven. This is the perfect Moon to set intentions around long-term plans and goals. This is the Moon of the purpose-driven leader. It's time to bang the drum of self-discipline and perhaps offer a renewed sense of commitment to something that requires slow and steady growth.

Capricorn is the tenth sign in the zodiac and is represented by the Sea-Goat. It is an Earth sign, ruled by Saturn.

Positive (High) Vibes of the Capricorn Full Moon

(*Set intentions for closure or completion in these areas*)

Seeing your ambitions all the way through to fruition
Taking responsibility & a mature approach
Finding gratitude for elders
Winding up business projects
Healing wounds around success and reputation
Finding completion with a disciplined approach
Recording traditions for posterity
Building your empire consciously and compassionately

Challenging (Low) Vibes of the Capricorn Full Moon

(*What you might intend to remove*)

Rigidity and sternness
Resentment
Not staying in the present moment
Touchy or sensitive
Controlling tendencies
Pessimistic attitudes
Fear of change

In Health, Capricorn Governs

(Areas of the body where you might wish for healing)

Bones
Knees
Joints
Arthritis
Gall bladders
Skin
Root Chakra (Muladhara)
Crown Chakra (Sahasrara)

Sample Wishes for the Full Moon in Capricorn

- I put away childish thinking in order to grow and mature.
- I am self-governing; I no longer need to take responsibility for other people's actions and emotions.
- I easily address my resentments in order to face life with eyes wide open.

Capricorn Full Moon Intention

I transform and transcend outdated belief systems and ego-based motives through honesty, acceptance, forgiveness, and compassion. I set myself and others free.

Capricorn Full Moon Healing Invocation

I sustainably achieve my goals, letting go of unrealistic expectations of myself and others.

Word to the Wise

When the Moon is in Capricorn, you are likely feeling ready to rise to any occasion. Depending on your personal constituency and situation, you may enjoy the stability and practicality that the Earth energy provides. But if things are feeling dense, fixed, or even stuck, you can incorporate elements from the opposite sign throughout the day to balance things out. The opposite sign of Capricorn is the Water sign Cancer. Consider Water-related activities to encourage fluidity: taking baths, drinking tea, making spritzes, using herbal sprays and tinctures, swimming in hot springs or a lake. It can be useful to combine the steadfastness of your intentions (Earth) with the flexibility of trusting providence to flow in at divine right timing (Water).

Working with Corresponding Elements

We suggest using one or more items of your choice from each element when designing your ceremony. Use as many or as few as you like.

CAPRICORN **Fire** items: Candles + Smoke

- Gray or black candles - trusting the unknown
- Earthy scented candles, herbal bundles, or incense:
    - Palo Santo - protection
    - Mullein - slower pace
    - Comfrey - healing
    - Patchouli - deep magic

CAPRICORN **Earth** items: Crystals + Stones

- Kambaba Jasper - higher wisdom
- Garnet - passion
- Snowflake Obsidian - healthy detachment
- Spirit Quartz -truth

CAPRICORN **Air** items: Intentions + Mantras

- Any personal wishes you want to make in the areas Capricorn governs + the High Vibe Aspects of Capricorn
- CapricornFull Moon Intention
- Capricorn Full Moon Healing Invocation

CAPRICORN **Water** items: Essential Oils + Flower Essences

- Patchouli - accelerated healing
- Nutmeg - intellectual stimulation
- Eucalyptus - cellular activation
- Bergamont - letting go of fear

CAPRICORN FULL MOON NUMEROLOGY

There are many ways to incorporate numerology when formulating your ceremony. You can find numbers to work with in the degree of the sign, the date, the hour you conduct the ceremony, etc. The Full Moon Numerology Empowerment Code is a special formula developed by Amanda Rieger Green,

MPH at Wise Skies. We like to think of this as part of our secret sauce. We use this number to find synchronicities as well as journaling on the day of the New Moon.

Capricorn Full Moon Numerology Empowerment Code = 5

Numbers have power. We add the numbers that correlate with the Sun sign and the Moon sign, to create a unique code to use in ceremonies. During the Full Moon, the Sun and the Moon appear in opposite zodiac signs. That means each one is assigned a number according to the Moon's zodiac sign and it's opposite.

The Wise Skies Formula:
Capricorn Numerology Code = 10
Cancer Numerology Code = 4
Sun in Cancer (4) + Moon in Capricorn (10) = 14
Reduce it down to a single digit: 1+4 = 5

The "5" Empowerment Code helps us see where we are unstable, irrational, and unaccountable. Notice when you see a 5 today: it's a reminder to slow down and get clear. Seeing a 5 reminds you to check your motives - there you will find your core stability. It can enhance your ceremony to incorporate 5 of anything in your design.

Numerology Code Journaling

- *Where do I lack accountability?*
- *Where can I benefit from an objective view with clear, practical thinking?*
- *Am I willing to assess my role in and let go of any chaos and instability in the energy of the Capricorn Full Moon in order to create more peace and personal freedom?*

CAPRICORN FULL MOON CEREMONY
Crystal Healing Bathing Ritual

The purifying bathing ritual in this ceremony invokes cellular rejuvenation and activates dormant parts of your consciousness. The crystals, candles, and essential oils help clear out any low vibrations in your energetic body, making space for you to move forward with peace and clarity. This is a wonderful ceremony for physical, mental, emotional or spiritual healing.

Pay it forward! This may be a ceremony that you perform unconditionally for someone else who is sick or in dis-ease (physically or emotionally). You can ask permission from the person and honor them in your ceremony for divine healing and light.

BEFORE YOU BEGIN GATHERING TOOLS, SAY THE FULL MOON INVOCATION FOUND ON PAGE XX.

Step One: Selecting Tools

Set up a Full Moon wishing area in a quiet space without distractions. Ideally you can do this outdoors, but a private space inside works too. Refer to the corresponding elements in the section above to select your tools. We suggest incorporating at least one tool per element (Fire, Earth, Air, Water), as well as a journal to write your intentions and responses to the journal prompts. You'll also need epsom bath salts for this ceremony.

Step Two: Ignite

Light a black or gray candle and place it nearby.

Say: *I activate the highest frequencies of the Capricorn Full Moon vibration, infusing them with my energy field to cleanse, clear, and purge anything limiting me from my connection with the sun light of my Higher Power.*

Step Three: Healing Waters

Draw a bath, by adding 1-2 cups of epsom bath salts to warm Water along with a few drops of the recommended essential oils. Be mindful of adding essential oils to the Water if your skin is sensitive.

Gently place a few crystals into the bath Water, stirring the Water counter-clockwise five times with your hand. Relax in the tub as long as you feel comfortable.

Shower Alternative: Turn on the shower and create heat and steam. Place the crystals you want to work with in the corners of the shower floor. Drop a few drops of the recommended essential oils into the shower area, creating an aromatic infusion. Stand in the shower and attune to the energies you've created. Relax in the Waters as long as you feel comfortable.

Step Four: Shake it Off

Use another cup of bath salts as a body scrub. If you are in a bath, drain the Water as you do this; whatever energies have collected in the Water have been detoxed from your system and must be washed away. Scrub your body from head to toe with the salts (be mindful of face and eyes if you have sensitive skin).

Say: *I am cleansing and clearing my energy field. I am rooted. I am grounded into my physicality. Any lower vibrational energies are transmuted into higher frequencies of pure positive potential. All aspects of me are here now.*

Step Five: Meditation

After bathing or showering, collect the crystals, candle, and essential oils, finding a quiet spot to meditate and journal.

Hold the freshly activated crystals in your right palm. Ask for additional guidance or insight from your higher self and spirit guiest as to limiting beliefs, behaviors and attitudes.

Step Six: Set Intentions

What is coming to mind after the energetic reset of the body scrub and new clarity from the meditation? Write any fears or lower vibrational energies that you are willing to let go of in your journal. Example: I willingly let go of _____. Next, write your Full Moon intentions, wishes, and healing invocations at the time the Full Moon is exact (or within a few hours if possible).

Step Seven: Crystal Enhancement

Place the candle you used during your bath/shower and your journal out under the Capricorn Full Moon (or in a window sill). Leave them out for three days and nights, allowing the light of the Moon to illuminate your desires to the Heavenlies.

After the three days and nights, retrieve the crystals and place them in your bathroom (on the side of the bathtub, in the shower or somewhere in the bathroom you feel intuitively called to place them) and leave them there for the next 30 days to reactivate the energies of the Capricorn Full Moon and your willingness to let go of limitations. They are a physical reminder of the intentions you cast into the Spiritual realm for assistance.

Bonus: Each time you bathe or shower, you can restate intentions such as: I willingly let go of _____.

Step Eight: Closing Sacred Space

It is important to seal the energy after any ceremony. Refer to **page xx** for our suggestion on closing sacred space, or say your personalized closing prayers.

MAKING IT PERSONAL

Moon Musings

- Amanda

The Full Moon in Capricorn usually hits my 7thth or 8ᵗʰ house, thus my focus is usually letting go of self-limiting attitudes and beliefs around relationships/partnerships or issues around power/transformation. Either way, this Moon always triggers insight around how I may be over-reaching, self-righteous, or too hyper focused on outcomes to step back and trust the process. I usually work to recalibrate yin (feminine) and yang (masculine) energies within myself. Here are a few moon musings from previous Capricorn Full Moons:

- May I practice greater patience, trust, and faith, one day at a time.
- Today, I turn my will and life over to The Power Greater than mySelf and the Highest Good. May I be of maximum service and empowerment to the world and to the people around me.
- I willingly relinquish control of people, places and things, recognizing that the only thing I have control over is myself and my attitude/perspective.
- I embrace my yin (feminine) energies of allowing healthy vulnerability to flow through me with grace and ease. Balance is naturally restored.

- I give myself credit for successful completions and credit my talents and abilities. I enjoy the fruits of my talents and labor. I am enough.
- My motivations are devoid of ego-based or self-seeking motives. My true nature is unconditional and to be of maximum service in this lifetime.
- Outdated patterns and unhealthy conditioning organically shifts into higher states of awareness and consciousness through my willingness to be open and teachable. I peacefully integrate life-lessons.
- I stand in my light and truth as I experience it today.

Best Wishes

- Tiffany

The Full Moon in Capricorn hits in my 1st or 2nd house depending on the degree of the Moon. So sometimes I add elements relating to ego/self (1st house) or values, money, and self-worth (2nd house). This Moon also squares my Libra planets: Jupiter, Saturn, Venus, and Pluto. Here are a few wishes I have used on previous Capricorn Full Moons:

- I feel a solid sense of completion with each project, knowing I've given each project my level-best - I'm ready to move forward to the next project with a clean palate.
- I willingly let go of all sternness, impatience, inflexibility, and defects of character in my mind and heart preventing me from the love and connection I strongly desire.
- I'm wiser now than I was before. I learn from my past, and embrace my future.
- I gladly receive recognition for a job well done and feel that my work has made a significant impact.
- Life gets better and better.
- All is well in my kingdom; I embrace a wise woman point of view.
- Above all, help me set aside what I think I know, and what I think I want, so that the Divine can flow through me. May I be of service to God and my fellows.

Aquarius full Moon

# WHEN THE FULL MOON IS IN AQUARIUS

When the Full Moon falls in the Air sign of Aquarius, you can expect some sparks to fly. You might notice extra energy, and advantageous personality quirks. This is the perfect Moon to tap into your inner Einstein, set a new intention to life the collective consciousness, or try something new. This is the Moon of the inventor and the free spirit. It's time to bang the drum of self-renewal and look at the world with fresh eyes.

Aquarius is the eleventh sign in the zodiac and is represented by the Water Bearer. It is an Air sign, ruled by Saturn and Uranus.

Positive (High) Vibes of the Aquarius Full Moon

(*Set intentions for closure or completion in these areas*)

Finding connection through empowering groups and friends
Finding solutions for issues that concern the masses: human rights, health, environment, etc.
Getting curious about what isn't working in order to find creative new solutions
Being radically honest in order to discover personal responsibility
Getting in touch with your inner weirdo
Finding completion with any area of life to gain liberation and freedom

Challenging (Low) Vibes of the Aquarius Full Moon

(*What you might intend to remove*)

Being overwhelmed
Aloof behavior
Self-righteousness
Being flakey
Judgmental attitudes

In Health, Aquarius Governs

(*Areas of the body where you might wish for healing*)

Circulation
Legs
Ankles
Heart Chakra (Anahata)
Crown Chakra (Sahasrara)

Sample Wishes for the Full Moon in Aquarius

- I easily connect with like-minded people to put an end to the production and use of harmful chemicals in our soil (or a cause you feel strongly about).
- I am willing to let go of any aloof or flakey tendencies so that I can be powerfully present.
- I am ready to experience improvement and with my circulation. I'm drawn to the right herbs, doctors, and natural medical team to help me experience a total healing in my circulatory system.

Aquarius Full Moon Intention

I think with clarity, act with focus, and behave honorably, while experiencing satisfaction and pride in our collective progress.

Aquarius Full Moon Healing Invocation

I was born wise, and accountable to a higher mission. I know how and when to take action.

Word to the Wise

When the Moon is in Aquarius, it's possible you are feeling pulled in many directions. Depending on your personal constituency and situation, you may enjoy the endless options provided under an Air-Moon. But if things are feeling too indecisive and scattered, you can incorporate elements from the opposite sign throughout the day to balance things out. The opposite sign of Aquarius is Leo. Consider contemplative yoga or something that combines thought (Air) with action (Fire).

Working with Corresponding Elements

We suggest using one or more items of your choice from each element when designing your ceremony. Use as many or as few as you like.

AQUARIUS **Fire** items: Candles + Smoke

- Electric blue, teal, or turquoise candles - conduit of clear energy
- Fresh and clean scented candles, herbal bundles, or incense:
    - Lavender - flow
    - Rosemary - trust
    - Olive - heart health

AQUARIUS **Earth** items: Crystals + Stones

- Chrysoprase -attracting abundance
- Botswana Agate - soothing
- Blue Calcite - mental clarity

AQUARIUS **Air** items: Intentions + Mantras

- Any personal wishes you want to make in the areas Aquarius governs + the High Vibe Aspects of Aquarius
- Aquarius Full Moon Intention
- Aquarius Full Moon Healing Invocation

AQUARIUS **Water** items: Essential Oils + Flower Essences

- Cypress - spiritual grounding
- Rose - love
- Lavender - calming

AQUARIUS FULL MOON NUMEROLOGY

There are many ways to incorporate numerology when formulating your ceremony. You can find numbers to work with in the degree of the sign, the date, the hour you conduct the ceremony, etc. The Full Moon Numerology Empowerment Code is a special formula developed by Amanda Rieger Green, MPH at Wise Skies. We like to think of this as part of our secret sauce. We use this number to find synchronicities as well as journaling on the day of the New Moon.

Aquarius Full Moon Numerology Empowerment Code = 7

Numbers have power. We add the numbers that correlate with the Sun sign and the Moon sign, to create a unique code to use in ceremonies. During the Full Moon, the Sun and the Moon appear in opposite zodiac signs. That means each one is assigned a number according to the Moon's zodiac sign and it's opposite.

The Wise Skies Formula:
Aquarius Numerology Code = 11
Leo Numerology Code = 5
Sun in Aries (1) + Moon in Libra (7) = 16
Reduce it down to a single digit: 1+6 = 7

The "7" Empowerment Code helps us see where we might feel isolated or lonely. Notice when you see a 7 today: it's a reminder to stay open to connection. Seeing a 7 reminds you to do a little research and investigative work, then share your findings with someone. It can enhance your ceremony to incorporate 7 of anything in your design.

Numerology Code Journaling

- *When do I feel alone or unable to connect with myself and others?*
- *Am I willing to let go of "my way of thinking" or a rigid point of view in the energy of the Aquarius Full Moon in order to experience more wholeness and connectedness to the collective?*

AQUARIUS FULL MOON CEREMONY
Ancient Alchemy

This ceremony helps you turn frustrations into pure, positive potential through alchemy and intention. Trust that you are shifting any lower or darker energies into something beautiful, abundant and intelligent while activating your wishes in the Universal prayer field. This ceremony is ideal for groups, businesses or setting the stage for healthy partnerships.

BEFORE YOU BEGIN GATHERING TOOLS, SAY THE FULL MOON INVOCATION FOUND ON PAGE XX.

Step One: Selecting Tools

Set up a Full Moon wishing area in a quiet space without distractions. Ideally you can do this outdoors, but a private space inside works too. Refer to the corresponding elements in the section above to select your tools. We suggest incorporating at least one tool per element (Fire, Earth, Air, Water), as well as a journal to write your intentions and responses to the journal prompts. You'll also want a soothing tea like cava cava or lavender, plus some agave or natural sweetener.

Step Two: Fan the Flame of Genius

Gather your ceremony tools and play some inspiring meditation music to set the vibe.

Light a teal, turquoise, or light blue candle. The candle will remain lit for the entire ceremony. Leave a few inches of space around the candle, as we will be building a small circular grid around it.

Drop a few drops of essential oils on your left index finger. Gently rub the essential oil on your left temple and then right temple. Add more oil on your left index finger, then rub the oil behind the left earlobe and then the right. Repeat this on the left clavicle area and the right. If there is anywhere else you intuitively want to dab the oil, go ahead. Be mindful of the eyes or any sensitive skin issues.

Pro tip: the left side of your body is a "receiving" energy side; the right side of your body is a "giving" energy side.

Say: *I am alive and awake. I am tapping into my innate wisdom, genius mind, and the intelligence of the universe past, present, and future. And so it is.*

Use your breath as a rhythmic tool to quiet the mind. Deeply inhale and exhale three times to create a natural flow and harmonic cadence. Meditate for seven minutes (Aquarius Full Moon Numerology Empowerment Code = 7). Allow thoughts to come and go as you focus only on the breath.

Step Three: Sweet Release

Take some time to journal any thoughts, ideas, colors or visions that arose during your meditation. Write down anything you are willing to let go of that is limiting you, including beliefs, behaviors, attitudes, or toxic environments. Write about anything that has completed or outlived its purpose in your life.

Read the Aquarius intention, suggested intentions, and numerology empowerment code to ignite the essence of the Aquarius energy and inspire your spirit. If one resonates with you strongly, go ahead and read it multiple times to really soak in the energy of the words.

With this new perspective, write your Full Moon intentions, wishes, and healing invocations at the time the Full Moon is exact (or within a few hours if possible).

On a separate piece of paper, list any limitations that you are now willing to transmute into pure potential and light. Once you have completed this, pour 1-2 teaspoons of honey or agave over your paper. Make sure you leave some leftover agave/sweetener in its container for later use. As you pour:

Say: *I honor these thoughts, experiences, and outmoded energies and offer them to the Sun to transform fears into love. I seal them with the sweet, solar light of intelligence. Namaste.* Repeat this three times.

Step Four: Seal the Deal

Take the (sticky) paper and roll it up into a small scroll. Gather an assortment of your favorite crystals and use them to create a circle around the lit candle. Place the remaining honey/agave, tea bag(s), and journal/additional intentions inside the circular crystal grid.

Using the flame from the lit candle, carefully burn this paper (use good judgment, being super safe doing this either out under the Full Moon light or inside over the sink). It's a good idea to have a metal bowl to catch the ashes.

Once the paper has burned, light a smudge stick from the flame of the candle. Smudge the area where you just burned the list by waving smoke from the smudge stick over and around the circular crystal grid.

Say: *I bless these magical tools with activated cosmic intelligence and invoke the alchemical process through all four elements. I receive a clear, futuristic vision for my life, born from heart-centered, pure, positive light. And so it is.*

Leave your magical tools under the Aquarius Full Moon for the next 3 nights. (Or, you can leave these in a window sill inside as an alternative).

Spend a little quiet time with your crystal grid. Meditate and listen for any wisdom. You may receive a brilliant idea, or you may not. Pay attention to any thoughts that come out of the blue over the next few days, as they are potentially answered prayers to your ceremony. Blow out the candle, but leave the crystals and candle in the same spot.

Step Five: Reset

After three days, return to the circular crystal grid with some essential oils. Anoint yourself with the oils just as you did at the start of the ceremony, however, this time use your right index finger and start with the right temple, then left temple. Put the oil on the right then left of each: temple, earlobe, clavicle, and anywhere else you feel intuitively called. Be mindful of the eyes or any sensitive skin issues.

Reminder: the left side of your body is a "receiving" energy side; the right side of your body is a "giving" energy side. Deeply inhale and exhale three times when you are done with the oils.

Step Six: Stirring up the Sweetness

Tea time! In order to use the tea and honey/agave, you will need to deconstruct the crystal grid. Gather the tea bags, honey, journal/intentions and crystals. When you brew the tea, stir it seven times if you wish to invite the Aquarian Numerology Code.

Find a quiet spot to meditate while your enjoy your tea. Write any new thoughts or insights that are replacing the outdated energies you transformed under the Aquarius Full Moon.

**The honey/agave and any additional tea bags you may have included are good for consumption any time after their ceremonial use. Know that they are activated with the energies of the Sun (Leo) and Full Moon (Aquarius) and carry the vibes of a bright, brilliant future—which will improve any peanut butter sandwich!

Step Seven: Gratitude

This portion of the ceremony combines the Air element (thankfulness starts in the mind) with the Water and Earth elements. Write a small gratitude list (seven items would be ideal). Burn the list in the bowl of ashes from your Full Moon wishes. Pour a glass of Water into the bowl of ashes, and use it to Water a favorite plant.

Gratitude is a key ingredient in this alchemical process. It invigorates a refreshed attitude, which prepares the path for a newer, brighter version of you.

Step Eight: Closing Sacred Space

It is important to seal the energy after any ceremony. Refer to **page xx** for our suggestion on closing sacred space, or say your personalized closing prayers.

MAKING IT PERSONAL

Moon Musings

- Amanda

The Aquarius Full Moon usually impacts my South Node(in Aquarius), hitting my 8th or 9th house depending on the degree of the Moon. True to my natal astrological evolution, I am usually facing challenges around getting out of ego-based motives (disempowerment) or philosophically detaching (aloofness) rather than connecting/sharing information. Here are a few moon musings from previous Aquarius Full Moons:

- I trust the uniqueness and quirkiness of my thought-processes and ideal and willingly and courageously share them with the world.

- I accept responsibility for my attitude and perspective, recognizing when I am creating a mind-set of disempowerment and fear. I am willing to shine my light.
- In the light of the Aquarius Full Moon, I comfortably embrace my Leo Sunlight and am willing to transmute anything that limits my cosmically brilliant light in the world.
- I see the future clearly, yet live in the present moment. I equally embrace and integrate my precognitive abilities into The Now seamlessly.
- I let go of detachment, aloofness, and uncompromising attitudes in order to allow a greater sense of unconditional connection, joyful involvement, and courageous mutability into all aspects of my life.
- All aspects of my personality and Soul-self are communicating interdependently for the Greatest Good.

Best Wishes

- Tiffany

The Full Moon in Aquarius hits in my 2nd or 3rd house depending on the degree of the Moon. So sometimes I add elements relating to money and self-worth (2nd house) or communications and writing (3rd house). This Moon squares all of my Scorpio-planets: Mercury, Moon, Sun, and Uranus. Here are a few wishes I have used on previous Aquarius Full Moons:

- I implement my big ideas wisely; I no longer feel overwhelmed.
- I'm willing to not squander any more time thinking too far ahead, so that I can be more present with the people in my life.
- I find myself with groups of people that share like-minded values; we help each other co-create interesting projects.
- I'm not playing small; my purpose is part of something much bigger.
- I invoke healing in my heart and crown chakras, putting an end to suffering and sacrifice.
- Above all, help me set aside what I think I know, and what I think I want, so that the Divine can flow through me. May I be of service to God and my fellows.

Pisces full Moon

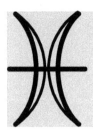

WHEN THE FULL MOON IS IN PISCES

When the Full Moon falls in the Water sign of Pisces, you can expect to experience heightened empathy. You might notice yourself feeling more teary and compassionate than usual. This is the perfect Moon to initiate a charitable project, to start new lessons in the arts or music, or increase your spiritual gifts. This is the Moon of the Mystic, and the Giver. It's time to bang the drum of self-assurance and look at the world with kindness.

Pisces is the twelfth sign in the zodiac and is represented by two Fish. It is a Water sign, ruled by Jupiter and Neptune.

Positive (High) Vibes of the Pisces New Moon

(Set intentions for closure or completion in these areas)

Finding compassion with something that has come full circle
Healthy boundaries with charitable contributions of time and energy
Finishing an inspiring book or movie series
Putting the finishing touches on a work of art
Listening to your intuition
Finding closure through meditation
Detoxifying mind, body, and living spaces

Challenging (Low) Vibes of the Pisces New Moon

(What you might intend to remove)

Taking on too much
Toxic environments
Unhealthy boundaries (or lack thereof)
Depression or sadness
Escapism
Addiction
Delusional thinking

In Health, Pisces Governs

(Areas of the body where you might wish for healing)

Feet and toes
Lymphatic system
Sacral Chakra (Svadhisthana)
Solar Plexus (Manipura)

Sample Wishes for the Full Moon in Pisces

- I am ready to remove all toxins from my environment.
- I no longer feel the need to take on too much.
- I face life with eyes wide open; I no longer need to escape.

Pisces Full Moon Intention

I feel whole and experience the alignment of my mind, body, emotions, and soul-self, letting go of insecurities that limit my faith. I am complete.

Pisces Full Moon Healing Invocation

I feel empowered and strong through rigorous honesty and healthy vulnerability.

Word to the Wise

When the Moon is in Pisces it's possible you are feeling heightened emotions, increased intuition, and more empathetic. Depending on your personal constituency and situation, you may enjoy the emotional depth provided under a Water-Moon. But if things are feeling too heavy, you can incorporate elements from the opposite sign throughout the day to balance things out. The opposite sign of Pisces is Virgo. Consider drumming, gardening, walking on the ground outside with bare feet, or visualizing roots growing through your feet to the center of the Earth in meditation to combine emotions (Water) with stability and practical outcomes (Earth). Combining Water and Earth elements assists you in anchoring your intentions with practical action.

Working with Corresponding Elements

We suggest using one or more items of your choice from each element when designing your ceremony. Use as many or as few as you like.

PISCES **Fire** items: Candles + Smoke

- Indigo and pastel blue candles - dreaming
- Floral scented candles, herbal bundles, or incense:
  - Sandalwood - spiritual grounding
  - Jasmine - spiritual awareness
  - Rose - loving kindness

PISCES **Earth** items: Crystals + Stones

- Blue Lace Agate - auric clearing
- Citrine - clarity and abundance
- Smoky Quartz - sustainability

PISCES **Air** items: Intentions + Mantras

- Any personal wishes you want to make in the areas Pisces governs + the High Vibe Aspects of Pisces
- Pisces Full Moon Intention
- Pisces Full Moon Healing Invocation

PISCES **Water** items: Essential Oils + Flower Essences

- Sandalwood -spiritual grounding
- Elemi - calming
- Ylang Ylang - harmonizing

PISCES FULL MOON NUMEROLOGY

There are many ways to incorporate numerology when formulating your ceremony. You can find numbers to work with in the degree of the sign, the date, the hour you conduct the ceremony, etc. The Full Moon Numerology Empowerment Code is a special formula developed by Amanda Rieger Green, MPH at Wise Skies. We like to think of this as part of our secret sauce. We use this number to find synchronicities as well as journaling on the day of the New Moon.

Pisces Full Moon Numerology Empowerment Code = 9

Numbers have power. We add the numbers that correlate with the Sun sign and the Moon sign, to create a unique code to use in ceremonies. During the Full Moon, the Sun and the Moon appear in opposite zodiac signs. That means each one is assigned a number according to the Moon's zodiac sign and it's opposite.

The Wise Skies Formula:
Pisces Numerology Code = 12
Virgo Numerology Code = 6
Sun in Virgo (6) + Moon in Pisces (12) = 18
Reduce it down to a single digit: 1+8 = 9

The "9" Empowerment Code helps us to see where we might be demanding, impatient, or apathetic. Notice when you see a 9 today: it's a reminder to get centered and align with your integrity. Seeing a 9 reminds you to pause and consider things objectively, incorporate a higher perspective and use discernment. It can enhance your ceremony to incorporate 9 of anything in your design.

Numerology Code Journaling

- *When do I feel impatient with myself, others or my circumstances?*
- *Am I willing to surrender the unreasonable demands and expectations of myself and others in the energy of the Pisces Full Moon in order find unconditional fulfillment?*

PISCES FULL MOON CEREMONY
Spiritual Detox

This ceremony offers a holistic and spiritual detox with a purifying charcoal and clay body cleanse. This ceremony is good for processing grief, ending a relationship or emotional turmoil.

Special note: Doing this ceremony on any Full Moon or at the end of a cycle (the last day of any month or year) is ideal to tap into the universal magick available to you for maximum closure.

BEFORE YOU BEGIN GATHERING TOOLS, SAY THE FULL MOON INVOCATION FOUND ON PAGE XX.

Step One: Selecting Tools

Set up a Full Moon wishing area in a quiet space without distractions. Ideally you can do this outdoors, but a private space inside works too. Refer to the corresponding elements in the section above to select your tools. We suggest incorporating at least one tool per element (Fire, Earth, Air, Water), as well as a journal to write your intentions and responses to the journal prompts. You'll need some honey, herbal soap, peppermint tea, and several tablespoons of red clay or bentonite clay that is suitable for bathing.

Step Two: Spiritual Soak

Draw a shallow bath (maybe 3 or 4 inches of Water). If you don't have a bathtub, no biggie! You can prepare a shower instead.

Pick an essential oil to use to anoint yourself. Drop a few drops of the oil on your index fingers, then dab the oil on your third eye, temples, throat, back of the neck, heart (breast bone), naval, base of your spine/sacrum (along your back), each wrist, backs of each knee and soles of each foot. Finally, drop some of the oil into the bath or shower to create an aromatic steam.

Say: *I feel empowered and strong through rigorous honesty and healthy vulnerability.*

Step Three: Crystal Magick

Assemble your candles (however many you choose) in a grid around your bath area.

Note: You can make a grid with any amount of candles. For example, you can use two candles diagonally in the front and back corners. You can use three candles to create a sacred triangle, four candles at the four corners, and so on. It's your magick to create! And it can be empowering to make the decision on your own.

Step Four: Muddy Waters

Turn on gentle meditation music, but consider leaving your cell phone out of the bathroom.

After you're in the tub or shower, mix a few tablespoons of red clay and/or charcoal with a bit of Water to make a mud-like consistency. Coat your body with the mud.

In the shallow bathWater relax and find a calm meditative state—spend as long as feels good to you soaking in the healing properties of the mud. If you are in the shower be sure to turn the Water away from your body so the mud sticks around.

Take as long as you want to soak and clear any disruptive frequencies or energies that are keeping you out of serenity.

*Option 1: If you are taking a shower, create your own steam room! Close the bathroom door, ensure your shower door/curtain are secured around you and leave the vent off for more steam.

*Option 2: Add organic, raw, local honey to the clay mixture for extra thickness, antioxidants and purification.

Step Five: Detoxify

When you're ready to clean the mud off, scrub your body with a refreshing herbal soap, starting with your face and going all the way down to your toes (being mindful of eyes and any skin allergies/sensitivities).

Say: *I am scrubbing my energy clean. I am transmuting any lower vibrational frequencies into pure light and positive potential.*

Step Six: Tea Time

Repeat step two (using the oil to anoint and ignite various chakra centers). Brew a cup of peppermint tea and pour a cup in your favorite mug.

Safely light a blue candle and move the meditative music with you wherever you are sitting for ceremony.

The Pisces Full Moon is the most intuitively focused Moon of the year. Give yourself plenty of time to meditate on your innermost dreams, deepest wishes, and most desired outcomes. After your detoxification process, you will have a clear energetic field and heightened psychic awareness.

Write about the dreams you have for your life and any intentions, wishes, or healing invocations at the time the Full Moon is exact (or within a few hours if possible).

Focus on the most vivid one of your dreams by visualizing how you would feel if it were true in your life now, using all five senses. Write it down in great detail. The act of writing pulls the dream out of the ethers and into physical substance.

Feel the energy in your heart chakra beginning to spin, generating a warmth that flows from your heart like a bubbling pale blue stream of love that permeates and fills the space around you.

Imagine 9 angels from the cosmos are standing in a circle surrounding your blue bubble of self-compassion, supporting you with serenity and love as you read the words you have written that hold your deepest wishes and dreams.

Close your eyes and feel the support of your spirit team in manifesting your wish. When you feel ready, give a spiritual nod of thanks to your spirit team. Slowly inhale and exhale three times:

Say: *All is well in my kingdom. I am the bearer of my own dreams and draw upon the wisdom of the Universe in unconditional fulfillment of my destiny. And so it is.*

Moisten the thumb and index finger of your right hand and then extinguish the candle with your thumb and finger.

Step Seven: Moon Cleanse

Place your journal and crystals under your bed for the next three nights. Set an intention to remember your dreams each night, then record them in your journal in the morning.

Use these three days as a period to be incredibly grateful for the power of your mind, the support of your angels and guides, and your health. Consider where you can offer random acts of kindness and write these in your journal to complete the ceremony.

Step Eight: Closing Sacred Space

It is important to seal the energy after any ceremony. Refer to **page xx** for our suggestion on closing sacred space, or say your personalized closing prayers.

MAKING IT PERSONAL

Moon Musings

- Amanda

The Pisces Full Moon usually triggers my 10th house and midheaven, essentially who I am in the world at this point in time. It always gives me pause to reflect on how I build myself up and how I stay small. It also creates an opportunity for me to examine my authenticity, asking: Do my insides match my outsides? Am I genuine in all aspects of my life? Do I see myself as the world sees me? Here are a few moon musings from previous Pisces Full Moons:

- I willingly examine my motives and actions with rigorous honesty and objectivity (non-judgment), in order to identify and detox all ego-based behaviors.
- I live with a profound sense of compassion for myself and others.
- My work and life's meaning transform lower vibrations into love and light. I joyfully create and articulate healthy solutions, peace, happiness, and higher consciousness through my life's work.
- I am clearly present in the world and responsible for myself.
- I let go of personal insecurities, face obstacles head on and trust my highest consciousness to divinely direct me, one day at a time.
- Gratitude and kindness are my natural state of being.
- I am love. I am loving. I am loved.

Best Wishes

- Tiffany

The Full Moon in Pisces hits in my 3rd or 4th house depending on the degree of the Moon. So sometimes I add elements relating to writing and communications (3rd house) or home and family (4th house). Here are a few wishes I have used on previous Pisces Full Moons:

- Chaos and confusion float away and are replaced with tolerance and kindness.
- Healthy boundaries help everyone feel loved and respected.
- I trust my intuition.
- I trust my feet to take me to the right place, at the right time.
- I can be helpful without losing myself.
- I am a drop of water in the ocean.
- Above all, help me set aside what I think I know, and what I think I want, so that the Divine can flow through me. May I be of service to God and my fellows.

"The real ceremony begins where the formal one ends, when we take up a new way, our minds and hearts filled with the vision of Earth that holds us within it, in compassionate relationship to and with our world."

- Linda Hogan, poet, academic, playwright, novelist, and environmentalist

Closing Guidance

It is our intention that incorporating these ceremonies into your personal practice brings you greater self-awareness, expanded consciousness, and joy. We hope that the ceremonies you curate will help you experience a profound life, and assist you with finding a deeper relationship with the divine within and around you.

These ceremonies are intended to be shared with your tribe and other spiritual seekers, in order to raise the vibration of our planet and the multiverse. This book is designed as a fun, practical and intentional tool-kit for quantum healing, abundance and expansion. Know this: you are a cosmic co-creator. We are spiritually connected. When you stand in your light with pure motives and intentions of bettering yourself, it helps all of us. Thank you for your work and dedication to your heart's evolution.

Our Final Prayer for You

May the Sun, Moon and all the celestial bodies in our solar system creatively and magically conspire in tandem with your personal magnificence to infuse greater love and intelligence onto the planet. Namaste.

With love and gratitude,

Amanda and Tiffany

The Abundance Codes Series

CODE: A system of words, letters, figures, or symbols used to represent assigned meanings. —Merriam Webster Dictionary

This book is part of the *Abundance Codes* series. Abundance codes are combinations of energies and characteristics that represent specific vibrational frequencies. These "codes" can reveal your biggest challenges and blocks while simultaneously offering keys for your growth and expansion through meeting those challenges. Abundance codes guide us in understanding how we may be limiting our experience, while also allowing us to tap into something much greater—a way of being more freely engaged in our own human and spiritual existence.

Everything in and around us vibrates at an energetic frequency. Quantum physicists tell us that everything in existence is made up of subatomic particles that are, at their essence, vibrations. From physical matter to emotional states, our entire world and atmosphere can be described in terms of vibrational energy. Different realities have different vibrations which in turn have different identifying frequencies. These frequencies vary in length and tone and make up everything from rocks to thoughts, from peanut butter to skyscrapers. Literally everything is made up of frequencies—including numbers. The numbers you were born with and the numbers that you live with are part of your code.

Ceremony is one of the simplest tools to assist you in your quest for more enlightened living. By understanding how to create a ceremony using the universal energies and elemental attributes, you can identify how their frequencies support or limit you. You will learn how to create abundant energy incorporating tools such as crystals and essential oils in ceremonies for your healing and personal development, as well as for fulfillment of your dreams and desires.

Creating ceremony for spiritual and physical abundance starts with healing false belief systems that no longer serve you, or planting a new seed with intention. When we begin consciously living with more intention, we start recognizing patterns and developing ways to align with the energy we wish to generate and attract into our lives.

The *Abundance Code Series* focuses on ways to understand and change your world for creating more abundance in every area of your life—health, vitality, emotional well-being, purpose, money, and relationships. In *Numerology For Your Home*, you learn how to identify the underlying energy patterns that you're living with in order to experience abundance in all aspects of your life. Once you identify what you want more of in your life . . . there's a ceremony for that.

Amanda Rieger Green, MPH, RYT

Amanda is the founder of Soul Pathology, a successful personal and spiritual development practice designed for individuals and organizations looking to create freedom, abundance and value through challenges by connecting to their greatest potential. She combines her corporate leadership development background and gifts as a renowned psychic with her personal soul journey through trauma, addiction, and depression—to expedite clients' understanding and practical application of their unique blueprint. Amanda is co-founder of Wise Skies Advice, an Astrology & Numerology business that offers developmental resources and products. Additionally, she is co-owner of Spellbound Publishers, a boutique publishing company representing authors who write in the metaphysical and spiritual genres. Amanda holds a B.A. in Religion from Sewanee, The University of the South and a Master of Public Health from Boston University. She is a certified yoga instructor and Reconnective Healing practitioner. Amanda is blissfully (yes, blissfully) married to Dennis Green. They live in Central America with their pups Tex + Abby.

Tiffany Harelik, MA, RYT

Tiffany Harelik (rhymes with garlic) produces books and podcasts in Austin, Texas. She offers publishing and publicity services through Spellbound Publishers and writes astrology + numerology forecasts at Wise Skies. Before her career in publishing, Tiffany obtained her Masters in Health Psychology and worked in corporate music event production. She is a certified yoga instructor, gifted medium, and world traveler. When she's not thumbing through vegan cookbooks, you can find her in the yoga studio, playing in her garden, or spending quality time with her family. Find her work at www.TiffanyHarelik.com

CPSIA information can be obtained
at www.ICGtesting.com
Printed in the USA
JSHW010728260120
3797JS00003B/27

9 780997 734997